T0353868

Barack Obama & US Foreign Policy

Road Map for Change or Disaster?

John Davis

authorHOUSE®

AuthorHouse™
1663 Liberty Drive
Bloomington, IN 47403
www.authorhouse.com
Phone: 1-800-839-8640

First published by AuthorHouse 8/20/2009

ISBN: 978-1-4490-0582-5 (sc)

Printed in the United States of America
Bloomington, Indiana

This book is printed on acid-free paper.

TABLE OF CONTENTS

Introduction

The historic election of Barack Obama as the 44th President of the United States represents an opportunity to shift from the unsettled and controversial policies that marked President George W. Bush's stewardship of US foreign policy. There is a near universal perception that Obama's message of hope and optimism will supplant the politics of fear that governed US foreign policy since the 9/11 attacks. However, a question begs: How does hope translate in international affairs? Additionally, how do we characterize the evolution of Barack Obama's knowledge of US foreign policy? Significantly, has that evolution brought him to a point whereby he can manage the diverse set of foreign policy issues that confront the new president during a period of war? The opening portion of this introduction provides the reader with a brief review of Obama's foreign policy evolution, followed by the strengths and weakness that emerged after the conclusion of the presidential election. Finally, the introduction concludes with an assessment of the issues that demonstrate the opportunities for a change in the direction of US foreign policy, and a separate set of issues, that if mishandled, that could produce a presidential tenure marked by disaster.

Obama's Evolution In Foreign Policy Knowledge

On numerous occasions throughout the presidential campaign, much like on the domestic front, Obama's magical oratory skills symbolized his intensions to reorient US foreign policy formerly guided by a unilateralist impulse to one governed by liberal internationalist traditions. Implicit in most of his foreign policy addresses concerned the need for hope and an accompanying word: optimism.

In the candidates' address to The Chicago Council on Global Affairs on April 27, 2007 Obama observed that as the world's singular great power, how we lead is a critical barometer in determining the world's respect for the United States: "Many around the world are disappointed with our actions. And many in our own country have come to doubt either our wisdom or our capacity to shape events beyond our borders. Some have even suggested that America's time has passed."[1] In a sweeping and declarative statement Obama made it clear that a new era is US foreign policy is emerging.

So I reject the notion that the American moment has passed. I dismiss the cynics who say that this new century cannot be another when, in the words of President Franklin Roosevelt, we lead the world in battling immediate evils and promoting the ultimate good. I still believe that America is the last, best hope of Earth. We just have to show the world why this is so. This President may occupy the White House, but for the last six years the position of leader of the free the world has remained open. And it's time to fill that role once more.[2]

This statement represented the first of many addresses that would flesh out his vision, a vision driven by high-minded idealism and hope. The address would later serve another purpose: it would be used by the campaign to identify the clear choice between Obama and the so-called Bush clone Senator John McCain.

For the Obama campaign the speech had another consequence. That is for the media, and among elements of the Democratic Party establishment, a question swirled quietly in the background: could Obama manage the always difficult and fluid demands of foreign policy where issues are often shaped by rouge states and transnational entities. In the view of senior foreign advisors within the Obama campaign the answer was a resounding yes. To deal with the remaining detractors the campaign planned future addresses.

In a clear demonstration of his self confidence, Obama ventured into the Aberdeen proving grounds of American foreign policy: he penning an article in *Foreign Affairs*. Senator Obama used the journal to further illustrate his competence in foreign policy. The subject of Obama's essay was "Renewing American Leadership." In what the campaign viewed as the most authoritative statement that identified Obama's objective of changing the course of US leadership, the senator offered these words:

Today we are again called to provide visionary leadership. This century's threats are at least as dangerous as and in some ways more complex than those we have confronted in the past. They come from weapons that can kill on a mass scale and from global terrorists who respond to alienation or perceived injustice with murderous nihilism. They come from rogue states allied to terrorists and from rising powers that could challenge both America and the international foundation of liberal democracy. They come from weak states that cannot control their territory or provide for their people. And they come from a warming planet that will spur new diseases, spawn more devastating natural disasters, and catalyze deadly conflicts. To recognize the number and complexity of these threats is not to give way to pessimism. Rather, it is a call to action. These threats demand a new vision of leadership in the twenty-first century—a vision that draws from the past but is not bound by outdated thinking.[3]

This statement is very much consistent with words used in Barack Obama's domestic speeches: he tells a story. Unlike his Chicago address, Senator Obama's foreign policy article induced criticism from liberal and conservative quarters. On the left, in a piquant critique of the article Amitai Etzioni observed the senator's essay proved to be "vacuous." Moreover, according to Etzioni, "Obama's favorite term, repeated *ad nauseum, ad infinitum,* is vision. What we need, the Senator writes, is "vision." What we need is a "visionary leadership" and "a new vision of leadership." This is, of course, all too true but also tells us very little as to which vision of foreign policy this new leader would ask us to follow."[4]

As one would expect the Republican's were dismissive of Obama's article. Interestingly, they spoke less of his objective to renew American leadership, but instead directed their response to Obama's criticism of President Bush's direction of US foreign policy. In one example, Lisa Miller, a spokeswoman for the Republican National Committee, observed: "Senator Obama started his career with a tone of hope but has quickly turned to one of blame" and "Obama has no foreign policy experience, therefore has no record of having done anything."[5]

Throughout much of the rest of Democratic Presidential Primary foreign policy took a backseat to domestic issues. When the subject of foreign policy did surface the comments among the Democratic presidential hopefuls proved to be haphazard and they lacked substance. That said Obama repeatedly had to deal with characterizations that he lacked experience or made statements that proved to be counterproductive. For example, Senator Hillary Clinton responded to Obama's statement that he would target Pakistan if "actionable intelligence" existed and if the Pakistani government failed to launch an attack on Al Qaeda safe havens in the country. According to Clinton, "You can think big but remember, you should not always say everything you think if you are running for president, because it can have consequences across the world and we do not need that right now." In another statement made in an *MSNBC* debate, Clinton opined "Last summer, he basically threatened to bomb Pakistan, which I don't think was a particularly wise position to take." In response, Obama stated "I find it amusing that those who helped authorize and engineer the biggest foreign policy disaster in our generation are now criticizing me for making sure that we are on the right battlefield and not the wrong battlefield in the war against terrorism. If we have actionable intelligence on al Qaeda operatives, including [Osama] bin Laden, and President Musharraf can not act, then we should."[6]

There was another memorable moment involving foreign policy in the Democratic Primary. The issue again returned to Obama's experience. Rather than launching another verbal assault Senator Clinton used a political ad to get her point across.

> It's 3:00 a.m. and your children are asleep," the voice over says. "There's a phone in the White House, and it's ringing. Something is happening in the world. Your vote will decide who answers that call. Whether someone knows the world's leaders, knows the military, someone tested and ready to lead. It's 3 a.m. and your children are safe and asleep. Who do you want answering the phone?"[7]

The ad proved effective. On the issue of commander-in-chief Obama's polls numbers were less than stellar. In subsequent rally's Senator Clinton would repeatedly use the ad to attack Obama's inexperience. There is little doubt in the short term the ad hurt Obama. Throughout the period of the political ad the Obama campaign countered it represented nothing more than a return to the politics of fear, which is something Obama believed is reminiscent of President Bush's 2004 reelection strategy. In time the shrewd Obama campaign came out with their version of the 3:00 a.m. commercial:

> It's 3 a.m. and your children are safe and asleep. But there's a phone ringing in the White House. Something's happening in the world. When that call gets answered, shouldn't the president be the one—the only one—who had judgment and courage to oppose the

Iraq war from the start... Who understood the REAL threat to America was al Qaeda, in Afghanistan, not Iraq. Who led the effort to secure loose nuclear weapons around the globe? In a dangerous world, it's judgment that matters. I'm Barack Obama and I approved this message.[8]

The commercial did not have national appeal, but for political observers the ad is important because of the message that it delivered: candidate Obama will respond to attacks that he lacked resolve or that he was unprepared to defend the United States.

As the primary process neared its conclusion, and with Obama all but certain to become the first African American to represent a major party for president, McCain took aim at the senator from Illinois. The thrust of McCain's criticism is that Obama's campaign pledge to withdraw US combat forces from Iraq, a pledge that undermined the "surge strategy," is one that could prove disastrous to the security gains made across Iraq. Second, on a grander scale, McCain believed that Obama is not the man to be trusted with America's national security: "The question is whether this is a man who has what it takes to protect America from Osama bin Laden, al Qaeda, and other grave threats in the world."[9]

The Obama campaign did not respond to McCain's criticisms because they were too involved with the preparation for the next phase of the presidential campaign: the general election. In an effort to slow down the Obama locomotive, and the media perception that the election was Obama's to loose, McCain understood that he would have to make a clear distinction between himself and the African American presidential candidate. For McCain the issue of experience represented the senator's best chance to defeat the media darling, the presidential candidate that built a cult following among the American people. It would come as no surprise that Iraq would be the opening salvo in the unfolding general election.

In May of 2008 Senator McCain formally revealed his strategy: he questioned how Obama could talk of withdrawing US troops from Iraq when he had not visited the country and he had not met with senior US military commanders. In a campaign event in Reno, Nevada McCain's comments were more direct: "Senator Obama has been to Iraq once—a little over two years ago he went and he has never seized the opportunity except in a hearing to meet with General [David] Petraeus. My friends, this is about leadership and learning."[10] Senator McCain used the Nevada speech for another purpose: he condemned Obama's position for his willingness to meet with Iranian President Mahmoud Ahmadinejad without preconditions. McCain made this additional comment: "He wants to sit down with the president of Iran but hasn't yet sat down with General Petraeus, the leader of our troops in Iraq?"[11] The failure of Obama to accept McCain's offer of a joint trip (what the Obama campaign dismissed as a campaign stunt) to Iraq increased the pressure on the Illinois senator to announce a timetable on when he would visit Iraq. Again Obama refused to commit to a date of travel to Iraq. As one would expect the Republicans exploited the situation. Days after McCain's comments The Republican National Committee started a clock that tracked the number of the days since the last time Senator Obama visited Iraq in January 2006. According to Alex Conant, a Republican spokesman, "In the nearly 900 days since Barack Obama visited Iraq, the facts on the ground have changed dramatically—but his ideologically-driven position has not. When Obama visits Iraq, he'll see that he was wrong to oppose the surge, wrong to continue to ignore our commanders' advice and wrong to demand premature withdrawal."[12]

It appeared that McCain scored a victory, at least in the short run. In time, however, Obama would use the issue of traveling to Iraq to his advantage. Using poker terminology the Obama campaign had a simple but productive strategy: we will see you Iraq and raise you more countries. Translation, not only would Obama travel, he would embark on a foreign tour consisting of multiple countries with Iraq slated as the centerpiece.

From the Obama campaigns' perspective the objectives of the multi-state nine day tour involved the following. First, overcome the perception that Obama lacked military and foreign policy experience. Second, use the tour to establish relationships with leaders around the world that could provide photo opportunities that could be used in the general election. Third, expand the foreign policy debate beyond Iraq, from areas where McCain feels comfortable, to Afghanistan and the search for Middle East Peace, for example, areas the senator from Arizona owns no decisive advantage. Finally, the Obama campaign understood the trip posed a number of risks. Of those risks, from the view of Obama's 300-plus foreign policy advisors, what some described as his own mini-State Department, they worked assiduously with the candidate to avoid any gaffes that could be used by the McCain campaign.[13]

In the Obama campaign's self-described "something close to a president tour," where he would meet with the leaders of Afghanistan, Iraq, Jordan, Israel, Italy, France, Britain and Germany, they had a number of advantages which they used to their advantage. The most important of which is that the trip was filled with opportunities, one of which concerned media coverage. *Newsweek* offered this description of the trip: "It may well be the decisive one of his candidacy, especially with so many media stars—including three network anchors—along for the ride."[14]

In each venue he offered a different prescription of how his management of US foreign policy would set the stage for change and a more optimistic appraisal of the American image. On the first leg of the tour on July 19, 2008 Senator Obama offered words of praise to US military personnel in Afghanistan: "We're here first to thank the troops…. America is unified in being so proud of the extraordinary, brilliant, dedicated professional service that is provided by all members of our armed services."[15] In a critique of the strategy employed by both President Bush and Senator McCain, Obama reiterated his long held view that Afghanistan, not Iraq, is the central front in the war on terror.

During the third leg of his tour Obama met privately with the Iraqi Prime Minister Nouri Maliki on July 22, 2008. In an apparent victory Obama's plan for withdrawal appeared consistent with that of the Iraqi leader, who offered this perspective: "US presidential candidate Barack Obama talks about 16 months. That, we think, would be the right time frame for a withdrawal, with the possibility of slight changes."[16]

In another significant leg of the trip Obama visited Israel and the West Bank on July 23, 2008. On the controversial issue of Iranian nuclear ambitions Obama repeated his long held view that "A nuclear Iran would pose a grave threat and the world must prevent Iran from obtaining a nuclear weapon."[17] Similarly, the senator made it clear he would employ a diplomatic approach to prevent Iran from acquiring nuclear weapons. With respect to the always difficult Israeli-Palestinian negotiations, the Illinois senator made no specific statement about how he would approach negotiations: "I'm here on this trip to reaffirm the special relationship between Israel and the United States, my abiding commitment to Israel's security, and my hope that I can serve as an effective partner … in bringing about a more lasting peace in the region."[18] Following the conclusion of his meeting with Shimon Peres, the Israeli leader is quoted urging Obama to "be a great president of the United States."[19] As one would expect Obama thought Peres' comments were flattering and comforting. In a demonstration of support for a Palestinian State Obama met with Palestinian Authority President Mahmoud Abbas and Prime Minister Salam Fayyad to ensure them that if elected president he would be an "honest broker."

Upon returning to the United States the Obama campaign was euphoric. With the daily glowing press reviews from the American and International media Senator Obama could not have asked for more. Thus the media coverage, the positive reactions from the foreign leaders that had the opportunity to listen to Obama's message of change, and the foreign policy experts that expressed support for his ability to "manage" US interests, the outcome of the trip proved beyond the expectations of Obama and his campaign.

Within two weeks after the conclusion of the tour the Obama campaign had to confront reality: not everyone thought his trip was important. The American voter had a decidedly negative opinion of the candidates' foreign trip where the majority of Americans were "not impressed by Democratic US presidential candidate Barack Obama's much hyped trip abroad and want him to concentrate on domestic issues rather than foreign policy.... The poll conducted by *CBS* News found most of the voters are more concerned with domestic issues than foreign policy issues."[20]

The introduction of Russian troops in August of 2008 into the breakaway regions of Abkazia and South Ossetia reawakened fears of Obama's foreign policy inexperience. In response to the crisis in Georgia Obama stated all participants need to return "to a pre-August 8 military posture is a necessary first step to resolving this crisis, we cannot tolerate the unacceptable status quo that led to this escalation. That means Russian peacekeeping troops should be replaced by a genuine international peacekeeping force, Georgia should refrain from using force in South Ossetia and Abkhazia, and a political settlement must be reached that addresses the status of these disputed regions."[21]

As the crisis continued to unfold, and the threat to Georgia's independence increased, Obama shifted his stance becoming more critical of Russia's incursion and blaming President Dmitry Medvedev for a crisis that introduced instability into the region. Following mediation efforts from French President Nicolas Sarkozy, and a separate track conducted by Secretary of State Condoleezza Rice that produced agreements that called for a timetable for Russian troop withdrawal, Obama's response underwent another transformation; his third statement appeared to be consistent with that of Senator McCain who made it clear the United States stood with the people of Georgia during its hour of need. McCain's position included the call for a US-led diplomatic initiative and a massive export of humanitarian assistance.

Foreign policy analysts questioned Obama's lack of decisiveness. To further demonstrate how the crisis wounded the senator from Illinois the McCain campaign observed the crisis demonstrated that Obama is not "suited to be commander-in-chief." Thus after a foreign tour designed to shore up his foreign policy experience the crisis in Georgia undermined whatever gains were made. As the crisis dissipated the Obama campaign endeavored to spin the situation in a positive light. Speaking about the crisis on *MSNBC*, Susan Rice, a senior campaign foreign policy advisor, attempted to deflect any criticism of Obama with the retort that it was McCain that spoke irresponsibly and threatened to widen the conflict. Rice issued this statement to refocus media attention on the earlier statement made by Barack Obama whom she reminded viewers that his comments were consistent with the Bush administration and the NATO allies both of which took a measured approach. According to Rice, "We were dealing with the facts as we knew them. John McCain shot from the hip [with a] very aggressive, belligerent statement. He may or may not have complicated the situation."[22]

Licking their wounds the Obama campaign shifted focus, hoping to move the debate away from foreign policy. The campaign moved on to health care; the decision worked. Obama scored points with those American voters that either did not have enough insurance or those that had none at all. Obama received another gift—a major financial crisis that threatened Wall Street and Main Street—that forced McCain off message and changed the parameters of the campaign. This was the backdrop that set the stage for the initial presidential debate, one that originally was supposed to focus exclusively on the subject of foreign policy, but began with questions about how the candidates would resolve the burgeoning financial crisis.

During the Presidential Debate in Mississippi on September 28, 2008 the opening thirty minutes focused exclusively on the economy. Thereafter, Obama and McCain sparred over the future direction of US foreign policy. McCain as expected demonstrated that he had attained extensive knowledge of the critical issues, whether in Iraq, Afghanistan, the war on terror, or dealing with Iran. Throughout the debate McCain took issue with a host of policy positions espoused by his rival, most notably Obama's failure to admit "the surge strategy" worked in Iraq. Second, McCain focused on Obama's statement that he would sit down with Iran and other leaders without preconditions. On Iran McCain observed "We're going to sit down, without precondition, across the table, to legitimize and give a propaganda platform to a person that is espousing the extermination of the State of Israel, and therefore then giving them more credence in the world arena."[23] Obama wasted little time in response. He stated "without precondition" should not be interpreted as "without preparations." Obama added that not holding talks resulted in our enemies becoming more threatening. According to Obama "You know what happened? They went—they quadrupled their nuclear capacity... And they sent nuclear secrets, potentially, to countries like Syria."[24]

With regard to Iraq, avoiding any direct response on the success of the surge, Obama took McCain to task on his earlier comments about Operation Iraqi Freedom. Looking directly at McCain, Obama made a series of tough, hard hitting comments: "[John] you like to pretend like the war started in 2007. You talk about the surge. The war started in 2003, and at the time when the war started, you said it was going to be quick and easy. You said we knew where the weapons of mass destruction were. You were wrong." Obama made this additional statement: were you not the one who stated "we were going to be greeted as liberators. You were wrong. You said that there was no history of violence between Shiite and Sunni. And you were wrong. And so my question is... of judgment, of whether or not, ...if the question is who is best-equipped as the next president to make good decisions about how we use our military, how we make sure that we are prepared and ready for the next conflict, then I think we can take a look at our judgment."[25] McCain quickly shot back that Obama "did not know the difference between a tactic and a strategy."[26] This statement was designed to embarrass Obama, and in many quarters there is little doubt that McCain succeeded, but because the Arizona senator appeared negative and disrespectable polls taken after the debate indicated that Obama was the clear winner.

ASSESSING OBAMA'S FOREIGN POLICY COMPETENCE

Irrespective of the perceptions about Obama's competence in foreign policy few can deny that as the campaign concluded the president exhibited knowledge that he certainly lacked during the Democratic primary process. In a more substantive assessment of his evolution there is little doubt the Presidential Election of 2008 exposed a host of strengths and weaknesses. With regard to strengths, Obama's oratory skills resonated with the international community. His nine-day foreign tour demonstrated Obama's statesman-like qualities. Similarly, his message of change, that is his vow to redirect US foreign policy, is something the world anxiously awaited. Thus after dealing with the Bush Doctrine and the unilateralist impulse that dominated US foreign policy under President Bush, many regions of the world desired a shift, a return to traditional multilateralism. Second, Obama's world tour demonstrated his competence on critical foreign policy issues, whether in Iraq, Iran, Afghanistan, and the Middle East. Consistent with this point the tour permitted leaders in Britain and France and those in the Middle East with an opportunity to establish a productive relationship as well as measure the tenor of Obama's foreign policy pronouncements during the campaign. Third, the all-too-numerous Democratic Presidential debates educated a presidential candidate long perceived as a lightweight in the area of foreign policy. Fourth, beyond the spotlight of the ever-prying media American's missed a major development: Obama "went to school." The 300-plus foreign policy advisors worked extensively to "spoon-feed" different concepts and approaches with the ultimate objective of allowing Obama to select an approach that would enhance his extraordinary oratory skills and his charismatic presence. This education process is not unique to Obama; a host of presidents completed the same process during the presidential campaign. This is true in the case of President George W. Bush, President Ronald Reagan or President Jimmy Carter. At issue, during a period whereby the country is confronting multiple wars can we conclude the "schooling" of Obama is sufficient? The answer is best expressed this way: as with all presidents there will be significant on the job training. Unknown is the extent US security may be undermined in the course of Obama's educational process.

The same process that revealed Obama's strengths provided a litany of weaknesses. For starters many within the foreign policy community were astounded and alarmed with Obama's statement that he would sit down with American's enemies without preconditions. Many foreign policy experts assert that this may undermine, in the case of Iran, the principle of no negotiations with terrorists. It is often overlooked that Iran (the definitive state sponsor of terrorism) has provided weapons and training to its radical Shiite allies in Iraq thereby undermining Iraqi security and sovereignty. And there is intelligence that Iranian *Al Quds Forces* killed or wounded hundreds of US military personnel across Iraq. Yet Obama desires to set a precedent: a meeting without preconditions.

Second, perhaps worrisome to experts concerns Obama's "functional knowledge" of US foreign policy. This is considered by many to be problematic because observers caution that with the reality the United States is at war the slightest mistake can impact allied cohesion, permit an adversary to incorrectly conclude the US president is weak, indecisive and thereby lead to an unnecessary and dangerous crisis. In one example Obama's *faux pas* concerning a possible strike against bin Laden in Pakistan set off alarms in the Pentagon and the State Department, and most certainly inside the Bush White House. It is certain the Pakistani government was not thrilled with the statement and it is a sure bet that their anger was communicated to the Bush administration. Now that he is president part of Obama's diplomacy will involve smoothing over relations with Pakistan who regardless of the campaign rhetoric has acquired a mixed if not a negative image of the incoming president.

Third, campaign promises in the foreign policy arena are often eclipsed by the shear magnitude of the responsibilities and interests of the United States. Consistent with the previous point there is another reality: the US is not always the controlling entity of events around the world. President Bush who referred to himself as a leader that would confront a plethora of domestic issues quickly learned on September 11, 2001 that his chief responsibility shifted to the security of the United States. When a candidate, and eventually the office holder, fails to recognize this fundamental verity in foreign policy invariably US leaders have to confront a period of paralysis. This was true with President Gerald Ford after the *Khmer Rouge* captured of the SS Mayaquez and its crew; this is true of President Jimmy Carter in the wake of the Soviet invasion of Afghanistan or the takeover of the US Embassy in Tehran by revolutionary students in Iran. Most recently lest we forget that President Bush appeared traumatized by the tragic events of 9/11. To be clear no coherent presidential strategy on how the administration would confront al Qaeda emerged until the close of the month of September 2001. The perception around the world is the United States was wounded and did not have a credible response or contingency. In the case of Senator Obama did it not appear that he was unprepared to deal with the crisis in Georgia? During the period of the crisis did it appear that Obama was off message? The point here is that historically presidential campaign promises have incessantly been eclipsed by foreign policy events. If Obama does not learn from the aforementioned examples his administration may envisage a paralysis of its own with the attendant consequences that during a period of a war are too lengthy to discuss here. To be sure the consequences are not positive for the conduct of US foreign policy or for President Obama and his leadership skills.

In the pages that follow the author provides the reader with a sense of the issues that will dominate US foreign policy. At the conclusion of most chapters an assessment is made as to how an assortment of issues may overwhelm Obama's domestic agenda, and perhaps lead to negative legacy in foreign policy. This is a recognition that President Obama was elected with a mandate to fix the ailing economy is now comprehending that foreign policy is intruding on the already full presidential plate. Similarly, in select chapters the author demonstrates that while Obama may have campaigned on the necessity of a greater use of multilateralism; however, when US national interests are at stake there may be times when he may have to accept the necessity of unilateralism. On the issue of Iraq the author provides evidence to assert that a host of issues may derail the "phased withdrawal" of US combat forces. It is during this interregnum that a potential disaster may confront Obama's leadership skills. There is another issue that will become conspicuous during Obama's stewardship of US foreign policy: the war on terror will test the new presidents resolve in ways unlike the previous administration of George W. Bush. Finally, in the concluding chapter the author assesses the prospects for change or disaster in the conduct of US foreign policy during the tenure of President Obama.

CHAPTER 1
RECLAIMING THE AMERICAN IMAGE

For many commentators the reclamation of the American image began on the night of Barack Obama's historic electoral victory. These and other pundits, like President Obama, will confront a sobering reality: a historic election by itself will not supplant nearly eight years of virulent anti-Americanism. Similarly, while the world, like the vast majority of Americans, were entranced by Obama's magical oratory proclivities, the president's policies in multiple regions will dictate whether there is an actual shift in the global perception of America's image. In this opening chapter the point herein is to argue that President Obama, irrespective of his rhetoric, is unlikely to restore the American image abroad during his tenure. Additional evidence is presented to indicate that the management (or the mismanagement) of a voluminous agenda bequeathed to him by outgoing President George W. Bush, combined with the requirement to use force to demonstrate resolve in an early crisis, may serve to undermine Obama's objective to restore the twin pillars of moral authority and leadership, pillars he views are critical to the renovation of the American image.

PRESIDENTIAL POLICIES AND THE AMERICAN IMAGE

The subject of the decline of the American image is not a contemporary debate. Indeed, the involvement of the United States in Indo-China sparked a barrage of global criticism of American foreign policy. There were a number of incidents that symbolized the negative perception of the American image. During Lyndon Johnson's administration, the former president had to endure international criticism that developed in the aftermath of the My Lai massacre. A number of decisions further compromised the American image abroad. President Richard Nixon's support for the Lon Nol government increased US involvement in Cambodia. The new adventure in a second country in the region angered the international community. Many around the world thought it odd that while Nixon was instituting his Vietnamization—a gradual reduction in US involvement in the Vietnam War—but simultaneously the American president expanded US involvement elsewhere in Indo-China. The secret bombings in Cambodia, and the resulting civilian deaths increased world opinion against the United States. Additionally, the collapse of the government in South Vietnam, and the perception the US government betrayed of its one-time ally, symbolized the failed policies that increased anti-American sentiment. Finally, President Nixon's intervention in the infamous Salvador Allende Affair in Chile increased the charges of "Yankee imperialism" in Latin America and advanced open condemnation of the United States in many quarters of the world.

The policies of other US presidents resulted in international condemnation. A few examples are instructive. During the administration of President Ronald Reagan the government of the United States had to contend with the international condemnation over the decision to support the Contras and the covert war that resulted in the mining of the harbors in Nicaragua.

During the post-Cold War era President Bill Clinton is responsible for a host of incidents that continued the decline of the American image. After the simultaneous attacks that destroyed the US embassies in Kenya and Tanzania in August of 1998 President Clinton's decision to launch Operation Infinite Reach, a massive cruise missile attack designed to eliminate senior members of Al Qaeda's leadership in the mountains in Afghanistan, and a second strike that destroyed what US intelligence officials described as "a suspected chemical weapons facility" in Khartoum, Sudan. The intelligence, however, proved incorrect. The initial cruise missile strike missed its intended target: Bin Laden and the other senior al Qaeda members escaped unharmed. With regard to the second strike instead of destroying a suspected chemical weapons facility, the cruise missile attack resulted in the destruction of a pharmaceutical factory.

In the wake of the aforementioned strike protests spread across Sudan. During the protest in Khartoum President Omar Bashir led chants of *Wag The Dog*, a reference to the fact the missions' intended objective involved an effort to shift domestic focus away from President Clinton's involvement in the Monica Lewinsky Scandal. Globally the international community condemned the "preemptive strike" as reckless and without cause. In another example in the Middle East Clinton's policy of intermittent bombing of Iraq to force Saddam Hussein's compliance with UN Security Council resolutions, along with the draconian sanctions, did not sit well with the Arab Street, and with other parts of the world. Perhaps the greatest damage to the American image occurred as a result Clinton's Middle East peace negotiations. Clinton spoke of being an "honest broker" during negotiations, but despite his rhetoric critics charged the US president was too willing to pressure Palestinian representatives in an effort to secure an agreement, and failed to apply similar pressure on the Israeli government. Irrespective of Clinton's "eleventh our negotiations," in an effort to secure an historic agreement, the American president failed to secure the long sought after peace between the Israeli's and Palestinians. The resulting tensions between the parties, along with the breakdown of "confidence building measures," culminated in the Second Intifada that exacerbated already strident anti-American feelings.

As the aforementioned history illustrates the decline of the American image is a process that began long before the election and subsequent reelection of George W. Bush to the Office of the President United States. That said the policies of President Bush inflicted more damage to the American image than any post-World War II US president. The evidence to support this statement is overwhelming.

The evidence of decline of the American image under President Bush appeared early and often. One of the early examples is the discourse among neoconservatives inside and outside the Bush administration which focused on the necessity to reassert "the American freedom of action" in international affairs. This involved two core tenets. The first component asserted the United States would no longer allow international institutions, long held relationships with NATO allies, and those among friends in the Middle East and elsewhere, to constrain the use of American power. A second corollary pillar observed that no longer constrained the United States would alter the status quo, which meant, particularly in the Middle East, targeting those entities that resisted or stood in the way of change. Among administration hardliners the entities were easy to describe: Iraq, Iran, Syria and radical Islam. Collectively, these two components exemplified principles that Ivo H. Daadler and James M. Lindsay described as central to a revolutionary movement of an "America Unbound."[27] These radical changes in US foreign policy would invariably impact the perception of the American image abroad.

Implicit in this new freedom of action requires the need for unilateralism. Within the opening six months of the Bush administration the international community quickly understood the burgeoning "unilateralist impulse" that would emerge as the center of gravity in US foreign policy. A few examples are noteworthy. First, President Bush refused to ratify the Kyoto Treaty, and then he made the decision to opt out of the Rome Treaty that precluded American involvement in the International Criminal Court (ICC). Third, in a speech delivered at the National Defense University in Washington, DC, in August of 2001, President Bush announced his intentions to withdraw from the Anti-Ballistic Missile (ABM) Treaty. The international clamor in the wake of these decisions was swift: the collective judgment of the global community is that President Bush is "selfish" and "tone-deaf" and provoked an outbreak of hysteria and a new wave of anti-Americanism.

The decline of the American image entered a new phase in the wake of the Al Qaeda terrorist attack that resulted in the death of nearly three thousand US citizens on September 11, 2001. President Bush arguably obtained something no previous American president had enjoyed since the global victory celebrations at the conclusion of World War II: world support. The global slogan "We are all Americans" symbolized Bush's opportunity to use multilateralism to forge alliances, to prepare the world for a real global struggle against the scourge of transnational terrorism.

In the midst of Operation Enduring Freedom there were signals the administration welcomed multilateralism, but only to a point. After the collapse of the Taliban regime in Afghanistan, the Bush administration welcomed the NATO-led postwar stabilization force, but the administration would not permit the alliance to have control over US forces, or its counterterrorism operations in the country. The President, following instructions from Central Command General Tommy Franks, wanted freedom action, which translated into US Special Operation Forces, and the regular conventional Army and Marine units to have control in their respective zones to pursue Al Qaeda in the mountains or elsewhere without NATO restrictions. An understandable move, but one which upset many NATO allies, most notably France and Germany, both of whom championed the idea of Article 5, and coming to the aid of the United States during its time of need. Subsequently, both countries were infuriated when Deputy Secretary of Defense Paul Wolfowitz thanked NATO for there support, but dismissed the idea that they were needed in Afghanistan. Quietly the American image, at least as perceived among select NATO countries, was on the decline.

There were other signs the American image was under intense scrutiny. The source of the international clamor involved the US military detention facility in Guantanamo, Cuba. Within months of the opening of the detention facility the US government faced scrutiny from allied countries and human rights organizations which openly responded to the mistreatment of detainees. One of the most embarrassing moments came in the wake of the report released by The UN Committee Against Torture. The Committee urged the Bush administration to "cease to detain any person at Guantanamo Bay and close this detention facility, permit access by the detainees to judicial process or release them as soon as possible."[28]

On the matter of torture the administrations sanction of rendition and black prisons around the world further damaged the already battered American image. On this point the president's critics were clear in the rebuke of what they construed as a negative legacy:

> Inertia and ambiguity seem to be serving Bush and Cheney quite well in their effort to extend the practice of coercive interrogation. One of the Administration's enduring legacies will be the fact that the United States is now globally known to sanction and use torture. And the specific techniques that have been authorized, including water boarding, environmental manipulation and physical blows, are relatively well-known.[29]

Thus the twin issues of the detainment of prisoners at Guantanamo, and the attendant evidence of torture, routinely produced international criticism.

The Bush administrations preventive war, what is most commonly refer to as a war of choice in Iraq, increased anti-Americanism around the world (matters were made worse in the wake of the incidents of torture at The Abu Ghraib prison complex), destroyed the moral authority associated with the war on terror, and impacted relationships with critical NATO partners. On the world reaction to the US-led war in Iraq, *Der Tagesspiegel*, a Berlin daily, offered this critique: "The political, cultural and social point of reference that America has been, is now eclipsed in the eyes of billions of people. The overwhelming impression: an imperial power is doing what it wants, regardless of its friends and its foes."[30]

The war in Iraq destroyed US moral authority in the war on terror primarily because the administration erroneously articulated an Iraq-Al Qaeda conspiracy on 9/11 that it knew did not exist. While polls in the United States indicated the American people supported administration rhetoric, around the world there was overwhelming evidence to the contrary.

It is often forgotten how the Iraq War impacted the Bush administrations relationship with allies within NATO. Before briefly discussing the alliance infighting, it is equally important to note that rallies were held across Europe in opposition to the Iraq War. In France and Germany both states not only refused to provide troops to the US-led war, both openly opposed the introduction of the "use of force" resolution in the UN Security Council, a move that angered the Bush administration. In response to the Franco-German opposition Secretary of Defense Donald Rumsfeld exacerbated tensions with the following infamous remarks: "Germany has been a problem and France has been a problem. But you look at vast numbers of other countries in Europe, they're not with France and Germany... they're with the US. You're thinking of Europe as Germany and France. I don't. I think that's old Europe."[31] Across Europe the media charged the comments continue to affect allied harmony, and equally troubling the comments were consistent with an "arrogant hyperpower."

Turkey, another NATO ally, refused to permit US military forces to launch a war from its territory to attack another Muslim country. Elsewhere in the Middle East the so called moderate Arab allies refused to publically support the war. There were two other developments that illustrate the burgeoning anti-Americanism. The footage provided by *Al Jazeera* and *Al Arabia* increased the already active and vociferous anti-American protests in the region. Second, Islamic radicals, pressed by Osama bin Laden's message to launch a jihad against the infidel occupiers, flocked to Iraq and participated in an insurgency against US forces.

There is another issue central to both American leadership and its image: trust. The invasion itself proved debilitating to the American image, but when The Iraq Survey Group could not locate any Iraqi Weapons of Mass Destruction, President Bush suffered from the "credibility gap." Beginning with the release of the Kay Report Bush lost all credibility with the American people and the international community. There was another consequence of Bush's credibility problems: states around the world reacted with skepticism when the US president stated that Iran was dangerously close to constructing a nuclear weapon. His own CIA issued a report undermining this position.

These are just a few of the policies that affected the American image around the world. In a definitive statement symbolizing the impact of Bush administration foreign policy on the American image, Zbigniev Brezezinski observed

> The world rallied around America, presenting Washington with a unique opportunity to forge a global coalition. Alas, the foreign policy that the president forged became outspokenly unilateralist ("if you are not with us, you are against us"), demagogic, fear-driven as well as fear-inspiring and politically exploitative of the slogan "we are a nation at war." It ultimately plunged America into a solitary war of choice in Iraq. Because of Bush's self-righteously unilateral conduct of US foreign policy after 9/11, the evocative symbol of America in the eyes of much of the ceased to be the Statute of Liberty and instead became the Guantanamo prison camp."[32]

Of the all-too-numerous polls that examined world opinion and the American image, the Pew Charitable Trust Global Attitudes Survey, which was updated in 2007, found the favorable ratings of the United States "have declined over the past five years in 26 of 33 countries—including most of our European allies—and are particularly negative in the Middle East. A *BBC* International poll from 2007 is even more dismaying: A survey of 26,000 people in 25 countries shows that three out of four disapprove of how the United States is dealing with Iraq, Guantanamo, global warming, Iran, and North Korea."[33] In the face of the results of these and other surveys, the Bush administration still did not understand the impact of its policies. A statement by Secretary of State Condoleezza Rice is instructive: "We must do much more to confront hateful propaganda, dispel dangerous myths and get out the truth"[34] on administration foreign policy.

OBAMA AND THE OPPORTUNITIES TO RECLAIM THE AMERICAN IMAGE ABROAD

Barack Obama is not the first democratic presidential candidate that campaigned on altering the American image. In the wake of the Nixon-Ford policies, during the 1976 Presidential Campaign, then Governor and presidential candidate Jimmy Carter incessantly spoke of the need to erase the negative image of the United States around the world. The American image according Carter was shaped by the ongoing saga of the Vietnam War, the secret war in Cambodia, and support for a murderous dictatorship in Indonesia that slaughtered thousands of East Timorese, all of which contributed to the negative perceptions of the United States.

Once in office President Carter warned the world of the dawning of a new foreign policy driven by Human Rights, and that the policies of the past were indeed over. In the words of

President Carter, "For too many years, we've been willing to adopt the flawed and erroneous principles and tactics of our adversaries, sometimes abandoning our own values for theirs. We've fought fire with fire, never thinking that fire is better quenched with water. This approach failed, with Vietnam the best example of its intellectual and moral poverty."[35]

Determined to reform US foreign policy President Carter employed human rights to end support for governments that oppressed their own citizens. In the view of President Carter this approach involved two objectives: "violating human rights was wrong, and such actions failed to serve immediate or long-term American interests."[36]

Despite Carter's foreign policy objectives there were significant negative consequences. Human rights, while an important component of US foreign policy when used appropriately, President Carter's approach undermined relationships with Turkey, Greece, and South Korea, and worse, he did not apply the policy evenly towards the Communist orbit, and then imposed sanctions on right-wing regimes throughout Latin America (and elsewhere around the world, particularly the Apartheid regime in South Africa) had little impact on reversing the global human rights abuses. Equally troubling, Carter's crusade for human rights overshadowed relations with the Soviet Union and other hot spots around the world, most notably Iran and Afghanistan. The results were predictable: Carter missed the Iranian revolution and the Soviet invasion of Afghanistan. Carter's failure is a warning and an opportunity for President Obama. The importance of altering the course of the American image is a significant objective, but how you pursue it, in recognition of the impact of that change may have on relationships with critical allies, and awareness that US enemies may take advantage of your policies, is important. At issue, will the message be heard?

During his victory speech on the evening of November 4, 2008 President-Elect Barack Obama used the moment to remind the world the image of United States will undergo a dramatic transformation under his administration: "To all those watching tonight from beyond our shores, from parliaments and palaces, to those who are huddled around radios in the forgotten corners of the world, (that) our stories are singular, but our destiny is shared, a new dawn of American leadership is at hand."[37]

Long before he was elected President of the United States, Obama made the issue of altering the American image abroad a centerpiece of his foreign policy. In an address to the Chicago Council on Global Affairs on April 23, 2007 Obama observed: "There is no doubt that the mistakes of the past six years have made our current task more difficult. World opinion has turned against us." In response to the Bush administration's failed policies, policies that influenced world opinion against the United States, Obama, in his usual soaring rhetoric, observed, "This election offers us the chance to turn the page and open a new chapter in American leadership. The disappointment that so many around the world feel toward America right now is only a testament to the high expectations they hold for us. We must meet those expectations again, not because being respected is an end in itself, but because the security of America and the wider world demands it."[38]

In a second example, during an appearance on *NBC's* "Meet The Press" on May 4, 2008, Obama used the opportunity to criticize Senator Hillary Clinton. Earlier in the campaign Clinton remarked that if Iran launched a nuclear strike against the state of Israel she would "totally obliterate" the Islamic republic. Her comments, said Obama, were consistent with Bush's remarks: they impact the characterization of the US image abroad.

We have had a foreign policy of bluster and sabre-rattling and tough talk, and in the meantime have made a series of strategic decisions that have actually strengthened Iran ... It is important that we use language that sends a signal to the world community that we're shifting from the sort of cowboy diplomacy, or lack of diplomacy, that we've seen out of George Bush ... This kind of language is not helpful.[39]

Obama's statements aside, evidence indicates that long before he took the oath of office, at least in the short term, the world's impression of the United States appeared to shift on election night.

The world's view of an Obama presidency presents a paradox. His election embodies what many consider unique about the United States—yet America's sense of its own specialness, of its destiny and mission, has driven it astray, they say. They want Obama, the beneficiary and exemplar of American exceptionalism, to act like everyone else, only better, to shift American policy and somehow to project both humility and leadership.[40]

In the midst of the natural triumphalist euphoria, Ethan Bronner, the author of the aforementioned statement, quickly warned that there are realities that are likely to end the hysteria associated with Obama's rhetoric of changing the American image:

There is a risk, however, to all the extraordinary international attention paid to this most international of American politicians: Obama's focus will almost certainly be on the reeling domestic economy, housing and health care. Will he be able even to lift his head and gaze abroad to all those with such high expectations?[41]

There is something else: with opportunities comes the recognition of the necessity to separate the reality of the moment from the realities associated with both American national interests and the responsibilities of a great power. Translation no matter the president or the political party, in the defense of the national interest, the leader of the free world often introduces US military forces to protect those interests.

For President Obama US leadership or the lack thereof is of critical importance, if only as a first step to dealing with the anti-Americanism around the world. According to Obama "To renew American leadership in the world, I intend to rebuild the alliances, partnerships, and institutions necessary to confront common threats and enhance common security. Needed reform of these alliances and institutions will not come by bullying other countries to ratify changes we hatch in isolation. It will come when we convince other governments and peoples that they, too, have a stake in effective partnerships."[42]

President Obama gave an early glimpse of his "new thinking" or what some have called "Barack Obama's American Exceptionalism." In an earlier address during the presidential campaign, then Senator Obama noted, "We must lead by building a 21st century military to ensure the security of our people and advance the security of *all people*."[43]

By giving allies and friendly governments a stake in maintaining not only US interests, but the interests of the world, a reference that there are numerous examples when they overlap, President Obama "hopes" the renewed interest in multilateralism will help quell or significantly reduce anti-Americanism around the world.

Not to be dismissed President Obama asserts there are other decisions that could alter the perception of the American image. Obama's decision to introduce and executive order to close the detention facility at Guantanamo is a clear step in the right step, but a number of significant questions developed in the wake of this decision: where do you send "high value terrorists"? Releasing them outright is not an answer; we have released middle and low level Taliban and Al Qaeda detainees only to have them kill again. Are we willing to the risk major attacks in the future by releasing high value terrorists outright simply to placate detractors without a serious plan to have them jailed or tried elsewhere? Where will the US government house future terrorists? These questions represent many issues that Obama will have to confront during his efforts to shift away or overturn many of the decisions and policies of President Bush. But as will see there are far greater pitfalls ahead.

Obama's Bush Dilemma

At issue for President Obama is this: is the prescription for change one of rhetoric or does he have a clear set of objectives to reorient American foreign policy to ensure that the country meets its discernable interests while ensuring adherence to international law and established norms? Rhetoric promoting the need for new leadership is not a prescription for meeting the national security of the United States, nor does it assist in the reorientation of American foreign policy.

One thing that is certain to emerge for President Obama is this: In his efforts to shift to a determined and expansive form of multilateralism and diplomatic engagement across the world, the ghosts of Bush's unilateralism, or worse his "unfinished foreign policy agenda," will always hamper the new presidents attempt to shed the negative images of the past. Similarly, his efforts to transform US leadership will have its own enterprising dilemma.

There are numerous Bush administration policies that have produced international clamor, resulting in intermittent bouts of anti-Americanism. From the Bush Doctrine, the Iraq War, to the use of Black Prisons, to a failed Middle East Strategy, to name a few, these and other Bush administration policies will impact Obama's agenda and his efforts to transform both the direction of US foreign policy and the image of the United States. It is easy to promote rhetoric during the presidential campaign, but once you enter the White House the realities of governing are altogether difficult. For starters, replacing a divisive and counterproductive doctrine is in many ways easy to do. But change in this venue will emerge only when the new president commits to an Obama Doctrine; one that works and will thereafter help in making the world forget about the horrors associated with the Bush Doctrine (i.e. preventive war in Iraq). There is an underlying irony. If and when an Obama Doctrine is promulgated, if it fails, there will be those that will long for a corollary to the Bush Doctrine (a protest that will lead by the Republicans), a scaled down version if you will. Should this reality unfold, it will not erase the negative vibes associated with the "old doctrine." Unfortunately, there will be increasing pressure on the Obama administration to succeed, not just from abroad, but from the left wing of the president's party.

In the case of "black prisons," another post-9/11 Bush administration program, those that oppose torture will call for the swift closure of these facilities scattered around the globe. In contemplating the closure of these facilities one should anticipate a bureaucratic challenge from the Central Intelligence Agency. There is no doubt the CIA (particularly those in the bureaucracy that will make the case that there are many successes associated with the agency-run program) is likely to resist the urge to close the facilities. Many within the agency will remind President Obama that until the United States comes up with a suitable substitute to house and "interrogate" high value "rendered terrorists," the prison complex should remain open. The world, know doubt, will seek immediate closure of these facilities. Many NATO allies are particularly interested in ending such programs because a significant number of these detention facilities reside within many EU states.

The Middle East Peace process, whether in the form of resolving the Israeli-Palestinian problem, is another unfinished Bush administration program that impacted the American image. From the Mitchell Plan, to the Anthony Zinni Diplomatic Mission, to the vaunted Road Map to Peace or the Annapolis Conference, they all ended in failure. Each failure produced open discontent from leaders in Middle East and loud protests from the Arab Street, and even among NATO allies. With near universal agreement, the message remained constant: too much pressure on the Palestinian Authority (PA) and too little on Israel. In the final analysis President Obama (this will be addressed in greater detail in Chapter 6) will have to confront the always contentious Middle East Peace morass that will emerge as a major issue on the foreign policy agenda of the first African American president. No matter the "new approach" Obama will have to continue with the same statements of "too pro-Israel" until a Palestinian state is formally established. Thus nothing will silence the long list of critics around the world that clamor for a "two state" solution.

In the aforementioned cases, and there are more, Obama's efforts to alter the American image cannot occur until he instills confidence in the world that his approach to these and other issues are different than those proposed and implemented by President Bush. In many ways Obama will confront the most debilitating aspect of the Bush legacy (how the former president's policies affected the US image) represents a dilemma that will haunt his administration.

As difficult as the aforementioned dilemmas pose, there is another perspective that transcends President Bush's policies. The vast American commitments and the threats to them are potential dilemmas for Obama's efforts to transform, indeed reclaim the American image. The issue of military intervention during the Obama administration is critical to unraveling the extent to which the new American president will actually alter the global image of the United States. This can best be described as the "will he" or "won't issue." That is under what circumstances will Obama intervene or conversely what are the determining factors for non-intervention? This is a critical issue for a number of reasons. Initially Obama will have to determine when, where, and under what circumstances he will introduce US troops around the world. This decision, in whatever form, will set the foundations for the second issue. That is how will President Obama control domestic and international reaction to that decision? If, for example, Obama introduces US troops into Somalia to deal with the omnipresent piracy, or to end the failed state, questions will invariably emerge. For starters critics of this decision will question if Obama is engaging in Clinton II, a reference to President Clinton's failures in Mogadishu on October 3-4, 1993 that cost the lives of 18 military personnel and significantly damaged the US image. Similarly, on the international front there will be a chorus of critics who will see the intervention as nothing more than neo-imperialist impulse. Third, equally troubling the "intervention strategy or approach" will give rise to a "so-called Obama Doctrine," which, as is the case with most presidential doctrines, will produce its own detractors. Rest assured the American image will decline under this or any other likeminded scenario.

Notwithstanding the aforementioned issues President Obama can successfully alter some aspects of foreign public opinion against the United States. A series of quick actions can provide a "sense of change" in US foreign policy and ultimately have a residual impact on the American reputation abroad. One of those actions has already occurred: Obama's decision to close down the detention facility Guantanamo, Bay Cuba within a calendar year. Other steps could come in the form of resigning and then submitting the Rome Treaty, which governs the International Criminal Court (ICC), to the US Senate for ratification.[44] Similarly, Obama's campaign pledge to increase the US foreign assistance to $50 billion by 2012 is something that is clearly needed and long overdue for the richest country in the world. However, this move, and others like it, while important, will have limited impact on the universal dislike of some of the decisions and actions made by President Bush and previous US Presidents.

In the area of public diplomacy, deemed critical to addressing the image of the United States abroad, President Obama could easily improve upon the Bush administration efforts. To underscore the failures consider that in the wake of the September 11, 2001 the Bush administration made an important decision to increase the use of public diplomacy as a means to counter the inaccuracies and propaganda that has been and continues to be used to attack the reputation of the United States around the world. Having Colin Powell and Condoleezza Rice, and others appear on *Al Jazeera* developed as a significant decision to assist in explaining or to thwart radical Islamic efforts in the region from misinterpreting US foreign policy to their advantage. However, for whatever reason such efforts were curtailed and eventually ended altogether. In another decision designed to address the American image abroad, President Bush appointed his long time aide Karen Hughes to the position of assistant secretary of state for public diplomacy. Unfortunately, the action proved fruitless primarily because her actions were not coordinated and were not viewed globally as a sincere policy of an administration that did little to change those policies that caused or increased anti-Americanism around the world.

To provide a more comprehensive criticism of the Bush administrations efforts in the area of public diplomacy, the General Accounting Office (GAO) made the following observations. The GAO recommended the US Government "needed to develop an interagency public diplomacy strategy. In June 2007 the President issued a *US National Strategy for Public Diplomacy and Strategic Communication*." The GAO then noted that its evaluation of "the implementation of the strategy must be guided by strong interagency mechanisms that promote information sharing and better coordination of efforts. In addition, content should be based on sound research of the intended audiences, with messages consistent with US foreign policy interests. Gaps in research data, foreign language capability, staffing, and resources hinder the United States' ability to best target and communicate with key foreign audiences."[45]

After investigating a host of agencies (Department of Defense, USAID, the State Department) that had access to participate in programs designed "to promote a shared sense of democratic values and principles, and mitigate the threat to our national security posed by the spread and intensification of anti-American sentiments abroad,"[46] no discernable administration strategy emerged. Though the Congress appropriated $1.5 billion to this effort, it was clear the program was significantly underfunded and the absence of an interagency mechanism doomed the Bush administrations efforts. Equally troubling the lack of prioritization of the program is another indicator that points to the failure of the program.

For President Obama he has a great opportunity to revamp the program and permit it to become a critical component to address the reputation of the United States abroad. Two recommendations are obvious. First and foremost there has to be direct presidential involvement. This is critical for the second component: the requirement of "political knowledge and skills as well as communication knowledge and skills. US public diplomacy needs to critically assess [American] … policies from the *audience's* vantage point and red-flag two types of policies: those that appear to contradict stated US values and those that negatively affect the public in some way."[47] Because Obama is blessed with tremendous communication skills he could and should be the center of gravity of any public diplomacy initiative in his administration. But with a host of foreign policy issues on his plate, will he consider public diplomacy a high priority, or will a host of security related issues crowd out Obama's campaign promise? The answer to this question is central to any final assessment of Obama's efforts to reclaim the American image. In the short term the unfinished business of the Bush administration, combined with the responsibilities of a great power, most notably the requirement to intervene to protect American far-flung interests, by themselves represent dilemmas that will cripple Obama's effort to reclaim the American interest.

CHAPTER 2
BACK TO MULTILATERALISM?

In his definitive statement that indicated his preference to shift from unilateralism to multilateralism, Obama observed "America cannot meet this century's challenges alone; the world cannot meet them without America."[48] This statement reassured the United Nations and NATO allies that the "go-it-alone" approach of the Bush administration is now at an end. This chapter addresses two core issues: the prospects for successful multilateralism in the form of international cooperation on a host of security issues to include the war on terror, confronting Iranian nuclear ambitions, Iraq to name a few. At another level, President Obama championed the use of multilateralism to confront a number of non-security issues such as the global economic crisis, the HIV/AIDS pandemic, and dealing with global warming. Central to Obama's pivot back to multilateralism requires increasing the role of the UN.

Second from a strategy perspective Obama is likely to employ an approach very much consistent with that of President Clinton. That is Obama will conduct "a social work-driven foreign policy" that, like Clinton, will likely lead to unsuccessful interventions. Finally, Obama will have to confront a significant contradiction. In the wake of the Air War over Kosovo the US military, in the mission/operations where US and NATO military troops are engaged on the same battlefield (Such as Afghanistan), has not permitted NATO to dictate when and where the US can engage or bomb Taliban or Al Qaeda targets. Herein is the contradiction: in Afghanistan, Pakistan, and other areas critical to the war on terror, President Obama is more likely to follow a "unilateralist impulse" that precludes NATO or the UN or any other multilateral entity from having a veto in salient threats to US national security.

OBAMA AND MULTILATERALISM

Long before he entered the Office of the President of the United States, many scholars, pundits, and even the world's diplomats quickly jumped on the bandwagon, asserting that Barack Obama represents fresh ideas and an opportunity to sweep away the stains of the Bush imprint on US foreign policy. Spencer Ackerman took matters to a new level. He argued that "Obama is offering the most sweeping liberal foreign-policy critique we've heard from a serious presidential contender in decades. It cuts to the heart of traditional Democratic timidity."[49] Does this statement by itself justify discussion of a doctrine? One statement alone clearly does not add up to a doctrine. However, Ackerman provides additional information that he believes supports his contention:

> To answer these questions, I spoke at length with Obama's foreign-policy brain trust, the advisers who will craft and implement a new global strategy if he wins the nomination and the general election. They envision a doctrine that first ends the politics of fear and then moves beyond a hollow, sloganeering "democracy promotion" agenda in favor of "dignity promotion," to fix the conditions of misery that breed anti-Americanism and prevent liberty, justice, and prosperity from taking root. An inextricable part of that doctrine is a relentless and thorough destruction of Al Qaeda. Is this hawkish? Is this dovish? It's both and neither—an overhaul not just of our foreign policy but of how we think about foreign policy. And it might just be the future of American global leadership.[50]

The center of gravity of this new doctrine is multilateralism, particularly an expansive use of international institutions. For President Barack Obama there are many reasons for the requirement to shift to a multilateral approach to US foreign policy. The initial reason for the shift is consistent with traditional Democratic foreign policy. That is Obama incessantly spoke of the Democratic stalwarts as a basis for the need to shift to multilateralism. The likes of Franklin Delano Roosevelt, Harry S. Truman, and John F. Kennedy are critical to understanding President Obama's philosophical underpinning. In his article in *Foreign Affairs*, "Renewing American Leadership," Obama observed "At moments of great peril in the last century, American leaders such as Franklin Roosevelt, Harry Truman, and John F. Kennedy managed both to protect the American people and to expand opportunity for the next generation. What is more, they ensured that America, by deed and example, led and lifted the world—that we stood for and fought for the freedoms sought by billions of people beyond our borders."[51] According to Obama, multilateralism proved critical to the success of each of the aforementioned presidents.

The link between leadership and multilateralism is another pivotal component of Obama's foreign policy vision. Indeed one might argue that there is no blurring of the lines; one cannot exist without the other. In his quest to unveil his vision for a foreign policy that called for the "dawning of a new American leadership" and one shaped by a "multilateral impulse," Obama articulated that "Such leadership demands that we retrieve a fundamental insight of Roosevelt, Truman, and Kennedy—one that is truer now than ever before: the security and well-being of each and every American depend on the security and well-being of those who live beyond our borders. The mission of the United States is to provide global leadership grounded in the understanding that the world shares a common security and a common humanity."[52]

Third, another reason behind the shift towards multilateralism is that Obama wanted to reverse the unilateralist impulse that was the centerpiece of Bush administration policy in Iraq and the attendant impact that such a strategy had on the image of the United States. The fourth point calls for the alteration of American foreign policy and involves Obama's attempt to place his on stamp on US diplomacy. According to Obama, "The day I'm inaugurated, not only will the country look at itself differently, but the world will look at America differently because not only do I have the experience of working at the highest levels of government on foreign policy but also because the leaders of others counties will know that I've got family members that live in small villages in Africa that are poor so I know what they're going through."[53] The point of the statement is to illustrate two critical points: Obama has a sense of the suffering of the underclass around the globe and that second he fervently believes that he can work with leaders around the world to confront and eventually resolve many problems around the globe.

Fifth Obama used the transition period to increase the media attention on his vision for multilateralism. In a press conference at his Chicago transition office on December 1, 2008, that was used to introduce Hillary Clinton as his choice to be Secretary of State, the occasion presented Obama with an opportunity to reaffirm his commitment to multilateralism. In the words of Obama "The common thread linking these challenges [both security and non-security issues] is the fundamental reality that in the 21st century our destiny is shared with the worlds. From our markets to our security; from our public health to our climate—we must act with the understanding that, now more than ever, we have a stake in what happens across the globe. And as we learned so painfully on 9/11, terror cannot be contained by borders, nor safety provided by oceans alone."[54]

In the wake of the speech, the press was abuzz with coverage that centered less on Clinton's selection as secretary of state, and more on Obama's statements concerning multilateralism. Jim Lobe, a reporter for the *Inter Press Services*, observed that "In an implicit repudiation of Bush's unilateralism, [Obama] … also repeatedly stressed US interdependence with the rest of the world, noting that all of the challenges faced by Washington were linked by "the fundamental reality that in the 21st century, our destiny is shared with the worlds."[55] Obama, according to Lobe, provided more specifics with the following statement: "To succeed, we must pursue a new strategy that skillfully uses, balances, and integrates all elements of American power: our military and diplomacy; our intelligence and law enforcement; our economy and the power of our moral example," [and] Obama said, adding that Clinton's appointment should be taken as "a sign to friend and foe of the seriousness of my commitment to renew American diplomacy and restore our alliances."[56]

The opening six to eight months of the Obama administration represent a pivotal period in measuring the shift to multilateralism. First and foremost with President Obama forced to deal with his electoral mandate—fixing the ailing American economy—one should not aspect any major multilateral initiatives. Irrespective of President Obama's fixation with the economy, opportunities, albeit small, exist to promote his multilateral agenda. Here are quick and attention garnering steps that could be used to jump start President Obama's multilateral agenda. All of these opportunities are a result of decisions and actions by President Bush. The international polity expressed indifference and outrage when Bush decided end US participation in the Kyoto Protocol. During the presidential campaign, Obama, and even McCain, expressed that it is essential that the United States participate in the successor international agreement on global warming.

The second step may prove to be the easiest and most promising given the Democratic gains in the Senate. Thus President Obama may and some would say should announce his "intent to gain Senate ratification of the Comprehensive Test Ban Treaty (CTBT) and several other long-pending treaties opposed by Bush, including the UN Convention on the Rights of the Child and the Convention on the Elimination of All Forms of Discrimination Against Women. He will also restore funding to another Bush target, the UN Population Fund."[57]

These steps represent a significant irony. During the first year of the Bush presidency the administration made the decision to withdraw from Kyoto and AMB Treaty, "unsign the US signature" to the Rome Treaty, and instituted a policy designed to decrease US participation in the United Nations conference on Racism. As one would anticipate, the international community expressed condemnation, viewing each move as a trend toward unilateralism and a shift away from multilateralism. Within a calendar year President Obama could be positioned to reverse world public opinion in many areas that have increased anti-Americanism, and second, he will be positioned to install fundamental aspects of his multilateral agenda.

That said a question begs: what is President Obama's foreign policy agenda, and how will multilateralism be employed to advance it? There is little doubt that Iran, Afghanistan, Iraq, Pakistan, the Global Financial Crisis, Genocide in Darfur, Sudan, Nuclear Proliferation, are likely issues, though not necessarily in that order, that will crowd Obama's foreign policy agenda. Oddly, each of the aforementioned issues offers President Obama opportunities to employ multilateralism as the central tool to redirect US foreign policy. Before addressing some of the aforementioned issues, Obama will unlikely have the opportunity to conduct an extensive review of US policy in many of the above areas. The fact that we are at war will diminish the usual time allotted to this process. Instead, to borrow the words of Richard Haass, one should anticipate he can buy himself some time by using his senior staff to do some listening, to send "his secretary of state or others around the world to talk to people. He'll obviously have a succession of visitors to Washington as well, so there are various ways to manage the expectations."[58]

In an odd paradox President Obama should be mindful the Bush administration has in many ways set the stage for multilateralism. That is prior to the "surge" Secretary of State Condoleezza Rice, in recognition of the sectarian violence in Iraq, deemed it important to move away from unilateralism and shift toward multilateral diplomacy. Diplomacy, however, was far more pronounced in Iran. Many would assert that this may speak to why the Bush administration did not use military force, particularly in the form of a surgical strike against Iran to target its nuclear production facilities. It is for this reason that bureaucratically there were a host of institutions and people within those institutions that worked to bloc or as some would argue delay the use of force in Iran. It is with this pause that Rice initiated her diplomatic agenda in Iran and elsewhere around the world.[59]

It the midst of this bureaucratic environment Rice accelerated diplomacy with Iran through the use of third parties, most notably Britain. This information notwithstanding, the Bush administration, answering criticism of its failed Iraq War policy, did meet with Iran as part of a multilateral United Nations-led meeting. In advance of the that meeting President Bush "broke his own diplomatic embargo on Iran along with Pyongyang, the last surviving members of the "Axis of Evil" by sending a senior State Department official, Undersecretary of State William Burns, to sit down with his Iranian counterpart as part of a larger meeting including other permanent members of the UN Security Council and Germany last summer."[60]

During the transition period Rice appointed Burns as the State Departments chief liaison to Obama's transition team. President Obama should build on President Bush's efforts to establish a US interest section in Iran. Currently, the US Interests Section is contained within the Embassy of Switzerland, which acts as protecting power for the interest of the US in the Islamic Republic of Iran. By creating an interest section in Iran President Obama "will no doubt make it far less controversial for the new president to open comprehensive, high-level talks with Iran without conditions when he chooses to do so (possibly after Iran's presidential elections in June so as to avoid boosting President Mahmoud Ahmadinejad chances of reelection)."[61]

President Obama's video message on March 20, 2009 to the Iranian people during the Nowruz celebration represents another opportunity to restart US-Iranian relations. The message represented an opening round of Obama's efforts to alter the US-Iranian relations. Some of the critical passages in the message are as follows:

> For nearly three decades relations between our nations have been strained. But at this holiday we are reminded of the common humanity that binds us together. Indeed, you will be celebrating your New Year in much the same way that we Americans mark our holidays—by gathering with friends and family, exchanging gifts and stories, and looking to the future with a renewed sense of hope…. So in this season of new beginnings I would like to speak clearly to Iran's leaders. We have serious differences that have grown over time. My administration is now committed to diplomacy that addresses the full range of issues before us, and to pursuing constructive ties among the United States, Iran and the international community. This process will not be advanced by threats. We seek instead engagement that is honest and grounded in mutual respect. You, too, have a choice. The United States wants the Islamic Republic of Iran to take its rightful place in the community of nations. You have that right—but it comes with real responsibilities, and that place cannot be reached through terror or arms, but rather through peaceful actions that demonstrate the true greatness of the Iranian people and civilization. And the measure of that greatness is not the capacity to destroy, it is your demonstrated ability to build and create. So on the occasion of your New Year, I want you, the people and leaders of Iran, to understand the future that we seek. It's a future with renewed exchanges among our people, and greater opportunities for partnership and commerce. It's a future where the old divisions are overcome, where you and all of your neighbors and the wider world can live in greater security and greater peace.[62]

The Iranian response has been tepid. Long after the Presidential Election the Obama engagement with Iran remains a one-way affair. Ali-Akbar Javanfekr, an aide to the Iranian president, Mahmoud Ahmadinejad, welcomed the approach but offered this caveat: "The Iranian nation has shown that it can forget hasty behavior, but we are awaiting practical steps by the United States. By fundamentally changing its behavior, America can offer us a friendly hand. So far what we have received have been unfriendly fists. Unlimited sanctions which have been renewed by the United States are wrong and need to be reviewed."[63]

Critics within the United States charge the message ignores Iranian nuclear ambitions, its meddling in Afghanistan and most certainly in Iraq. While the video message is another important step, by itself, it is unlikely to transform a relationship that has been hampered by mistrust, dissimilar visions within the Middle East, and from the US perspective direct and indirect Iranian policies that have resulted in the death of US civilians (those that perished in the destruction of the US embassy in Beirut and the 241 Marines that lost their lives in Lebanon in 1983) and US military personnel in Iraq that were killed (via IEDs or other weapons given to Shiite militia's) as a result of the activities of the *Al Quds* Forces and Iranian agents that operated across the country.

For President Obama there are a number of additional opportunities that are consistent with the principles of multilateralism. But before introducing those issues it is important to provide a caveat for President Obama. To begin with, whether the left wing of Democratic Party and those that serve in Obama's State Department, whether they want to admit or not, the path to multilateralism has long ago started in the latter two years of the Bush administration. It is here that the warning should be unveiled: President Obama and his senior foreign policy advisers will have to avoid a critical mistake made by President Bush and the neoconservative ideologues. During the review of a host of policies whether in the case of Iraq, North Korea, the use of multilateral organizations (particularly the United Nations or the NATO), the former president and "the hawks" employed three letters—"ABC" or "Any Thing But Clinton"—as a way of dismissing the policy initiatives of President Bill Clinton, many of which were successful.[64] As the following statement by a senior Bush administration official demonstrates the ideologues in the Bush administration were not concerned with the issue of success:

> The part I noticed right away was that they had a great disdain for Clinton and his policies and by association anybody who had worked for Clinton. So they were ready to throw them out—the presumption was that Clinton policy should go, all Clinton policy, unless proven otherwise. It was sort of guilty until proven innocent. And that's pretty unusual.... The assumption typically is "continuity of policy" unless there is reason to change it. But with this crowd, it was the reverse .... So in that sense, they were very ideological or partisan or however you would like to describe it.[65]

In one of example then Secretary of State Colin Powell wanted to continue the "Sunshine policy" of the Clinton years. In a swift rebuke the White House reprimanded Powell for violating the "ABC" dictum, and forced the secretary of state to withdraw his statement. Thereafter, the sunshine policy existed no more.[66]

The test for President Obama is to avoid coming up with his own dictum: "ABB" or Anything But Bush." By proceeding along this path this be clear signal that his administration will conduct a non-ideological approach to US foreign policy.

The issues that lend themselves to multilateralism are as follows: Afghanistan, Iraq, the Global Financial Crisis, Somalia, HIV/AIDS, and Global Warming. Since the commencement of Operation Enduring Freedom there is little doubt that Afghanistan was a global concern. The military operation aside, in the wake of the collapse of the Taliban, and the destruction of the Al Qaeda training camps across the country, the multilateral postwar reconstruction began. From the United Nations, to the European Union[67], to Arab League, to say the least the United States, there is little doubt the world was active and attentive to Afghanistan's future. However, despite pledges and attentiveness from a concerned global community, the rapidly deteriorating security situation outside of the capital of Kabul, along with the Bush administrations shift to Iraq, set the stage for dwindling results in Afghanistan.

Oddly as the situation stabilized in Iraq conditions in Afghanistan deteriorated. With the success of the surge in Iraq, discourse on the future of Afghanistan reached a fever pitch, but what was clear is that the multilateral process was dissipating. In particular, NATO states were concerned that the counterinsurgency strategy had failed. The reality is that NATO efforts to increase troops resulted in a dismal failure. Equally troubling NATO members openly discussed the reduction and in some cases a timetable for the withdrawal of their troops.

Quietly the Bush administration, in spite of the new political realities in Afghanistan pressed the EU and other states to retain the multilateral process. With the Bush administration tenure over President Obama was left with an opportunity to rebuild and sustain the multilateral effort.

During the presidential campaign then Senator Obama made a trip to Afghanistan. The trip was spun as an effort to increase Obama's foreign policy credentials. Obama's statements were predictable: increase US troop presence in the country. Similarly, he warned Afghanistan, not Iraq, is the central front in the war on terror. In an appearance on the *CBS* morning program "Face the Nation" on July 20, 2008, Obama stated "The Afghan government needs to do more. But we have to understand that the situation is precarious and urgent here in Afghanistan. And I believe this has to be our central focus, the central front, on our battle against terrorism."[68]

President Obama now has the opportunity to save a multilateral process that is dwindling rapidly. How to save Afghanistan? While it is important for Obama to listen to General David Patreaus, the lesson from Iraq is that a military option by itself will not save Afghanistan. To win the "hearts and minds" of the civilian population a multilateral effort has to commence in unstable areas across the country. Once areas now controlled by the Taliban are secured, the reconstruction process should commence immediately. There are many factors that could hamper multilateralism in Afghanistan. First, the global financial crisis will impact the multilateral effort, reducing financial commitments by the US, the EU and states around the world. Second, domestic pressure and the need to remain attentive to Obama's electoral mandate will force the president to deal with fixing the ailing American economy. Third, sustaining the multilateral process will be difficult for another reason: the expected Taliban spring offensive could delay any major shift in multilateralism. Collectively, President Obama will be forced to continue to increase US forces. If there is a major increase in American casualties, President Obama will be forced to address a twin set of issues: change the American strategy, reduce the American troop commitment, and hope that Afghan troops could do the job (which currently they are unable to do). Second, during this period of crisis there is an attendant consequence, the momentum for a multilateral reconstruction effort will decline considerably.

The Global Financial Crisis is critical for President Obama. The president has correctly understood the realities of interdependence and how the crisis has impacted the global economy. That said Obama would do well do remember the lessons of President Franklin Roosevelt and President Bill Clinton: the significance of foreign economic policy. This is an area of foreign policy that receives too little attention. Both FDR and Clinton recognized that the foreign economic policy is critical to curing the ailing American economy and the world economy. For President Roosevelt his "New Deal" extended far beyond the shores of the United States, and it was critical to his plans to bring the United States and the world out of the expansive Great Depression.[69] In the case of President Clinton, though the US economy was in better shape than under President Roosevelt, he recognized that creating new and maintaining old global markets were critical for the long term health of the US economy. To assist in this effort President Clinton created a new bureaucratic institution known as the National Economic Council (NEC). This entity met much in the same way as the National Security Council (NSC) to coordinate foreign economic policy. Like Roosevelt before him, foreign economic policy became a vital component of Clinton's legacy in foreign policy.[70]

In the case of President Obama foreign economic policy will be far more important now than was the case under Clinton. Once again Obama will benefit from a multilateral process that is well under way. In the closing months of Bush administration the president met with the leaders of the G-8 and G-20 in an effort to confront the challenges posed by the Global Financial Crisis. The objective of the meetings was fundamental: prevent a global recession. Irrespective of the massive bailout reforms the leaders of the world failed in their efforts to prevent a global recession. During the course of G-20 gathering in White House, Obama sent representatives on his behalf. In the aftermath of his electoral victory Obama telephoned a number of world leaders, in particular those from Australia, Britain, Canada, France, Germany, Israel, Japan, Mexico and South Korea. There is little doubt the subject of the global financial crisis surfaced. Since taking office the multilateral process begun under Bush is now adrift. As one would surmise the global crisis continues unabated. At issue, will the lessons of foreign economic policy employed by two Democratic Presidents, and the multilateral process that was used to implement their plans, ever catch on with President Obama? If and when an extensive multilateral process commences one should not anticipate any quick fix. The global financial crisis will extend well into 2010, if not longer, and if President Obama intends to match the historic efforts of Roosevelt and Clinton he will do well to develop a long term plan that includes the major economies of the world.

One area open to President Obama to assist in stemming the global recession is to follow the path set by President Roosevelt. FDR's efforts to bring world leaders together to the Bretton Woods system that established the International Monetary Fund and the World Bank were each critical to rebuilding confidence in the international economic system. Roosevelt succeeded and it is possible that so too can Obama. Thus a grand multilateral opportunity is available for Obama to confront not only what ails the American economy, but far more significant, the global economy.

President Obama has been fixated on the importance of multilateralism. As he makes a determined shift in the direction of a multilateral international institution-based foreign policy, President Obama may well understand the perils associated with this path. The point of the aforementioned statement is to provide a warning, a definitive caveat if you will to avoid a major failure of the Clinton presidency: the use of "foreign policy as social work." Michael Mandelbaum offers this assessment of that era:

> The abortive interventions shared several features. Each involved small, poor, weak countries far from the crucial centers that had dominated American foreign policy during the Cold War. Whereas previous administrations had been concerned with the powerful and potentially dangerous members of the international community, which constitute its core, the Clinton administration turned its attention to the international periphery. In these peripheral areas the administration was preoccupied not with relations with neighboring countries, the usual subject of foreign policy, but rather with the social, political, and economic conditions within borders. It aimed to relieve the suffering caused by ethnic cleansing in Bosnia, starvation in Somalia, and oppression in Haiti. Historically the foreign policy of the United States has centered on American interests, defined as developments that could affect the lives of American citizens. Nothing that occurred in these three countries fit that criterion.[71]

In each case President Clinton intervened, and only in one of those cases—Central Europe (Bosnia and later Kosovo)—did he succeed. The failures precluded advancement of other multilateral issues such as Rwanda, which the Clinton administration avoided precisely due to the outcome in Somalia. This is a reference to the Mogadishu firefight on October 3-4, 1993 that resulted in the death of eighteen American soldiers. Interestingly, President Clinton blamed the fiasco on the mismanagement of the mission on the United Nations. Clinton thereafter warned that US troops would never again be placed under foreign command. The subsequent American withdrawal from Somalia resulted in criticism of Clinton's lack of resolve, and it damaged the credibility of the president and the US military. In the developing world many believed that if you killed a few US soldiers, eventually, because the American people had no stomach for major troop casualties, the domestic clamor would result in the withdrawal of American military personnel. There is another dilemma for the Democratic President.

> President Clinton's foreign policy, rather than protecting American national interests, has pursued *social work worldwide* [emphasis added]. Three failed interventions in 1993—in Bosnia, in Somalia, and the first try in Haiti—illustrate this dramatically. Preoccupied with "helping the helpless," the administration alienated vital allies, changed direction repeatedly to repair Clinton's sagging image, and let special interest groups harm US policy toward Japan and Russia. With his domestic policy stalled, Clinton's opponents may end up painting him what he never wanted to be: a foreign policy president.[72]

When used appropriately multilateralism is indeed a critical component of American foreign policy. But multilateralism by itself is no guarantee for a successful foreign policy. So when considering intervention, presumably a UN Chapter VII intervention, it is the objectives of the intervention, along with an effective military strategy that will guarantee success. President Obama's campaign rhetoric boasted of new leadership based on traditional American multilateralism announces to the world that the unilateral impulse is over and helps to quiet fears of an impending preemptive or even preventive intervention. But to those astute foreign policy watchers that paid attention to Obama's campaign a host a red flags should have been raised. Most notably he spoke of the need to shift away from unilateralism and a foreign policy dominated by dogma, to one guided by multilateralism. Consider this statement made by Obama

> No President should ever hesitate to use force—unilaterally if necessary—to protect ourselves and our vital interests when we are attacked or imminently threatened. But when we use force in situations other than self-defense, we should make every effort to garner the clear support and participation of others—the kind of burden-sharing and support President George H.W. Bush mustered before he launched Operation Desert Storm.[73]

In reading this statement a host of issues arise. First, how serious is Obama about multilateralism when he makes a statement such as this? Second, the aforementioned statement provides a clear indication that Obama recognizes that a president may be forced to act preemptively to protect US interests, even if there are occasions when a president should employ a "burden sharing" approach, a clear reference to multilateralism. The issue and perhaps danger for the United States is this: Do we know if President Obama will know which option to select during a crisis? President Bush's failure produced a war of choice that cost the United States treasury over $700 Billion dollars, an unnecessary loss of military lives, lost moral authority, and continues to impair the war on terror. Finally, there is a strange dilemma that President Obama will have to confront. A shift back to multilateralism under Clinton increased the use of force and damaged American creditability during his tenure in office. Sadly, neither President Clinton's image, nor the image of the United States abroad recovered. In a shift away from multilateralism and towards unilateralism, the American image took a beating after the preventive war in Iraq was launched. For President Obama a question begs: In your shift back to multilateralism can the American people count on you avoiding a war? Conversely, given that several wars are taking place can Obama assure the American people that he will not mismanage them? The answer to these questions will determine the final judgment of President Obama's shift to multilateralism.

CHAPTER 3
THE DILEMMA: THE SEARCH FOR A POLESTAR

Since the end of the Cold War a recurring debate dominated US foreign policy: the requirement for a strategic replacement to supplant containment. In the wake of the death and destruction that occurred on the September 11, 2001 Republican commentators remarked the Bush Doctrine provided the "moral clarity" and a new strategic instrument to guide US foreign policy. In Obama's assessment of the controversial doctrine he noted it failed because it placed the US in a negative position of "only speaking to leaders of rogue nations if they first meet conditions laid out by the United States."[74] With regard to his instrument to guide US foreign policy, Obama refused to be specific. To illustrate the point during the presidential campaign in what was billed as a major foreign policy address in Fayetteville, N.C. on March 19, 2008 Senator Obama made this statement: "What I have talked about today is a new strategy, a new set of priorities for pursuing our interests in the 21st century. And as President, I will provide the tools required to implement this strategy. When President Truman put the policy of containment in place he also invested in and organized our government to carry it out—creating the National Security Council and the CIA, and founding NATO. Now, we must upgrade our tools of power to fit a new strategy."[75] Thereafter Obama never offered any details; a critical opportunity to flesh out the details of the strategy to guide Obama's foreign policy dissipated without any subsequent clarification. Well into his presidency Obama has yet to move beyond the presidential rhetoric.

In this chapter the author asserts President Obama is likely to follow the dangerous approach supplied by the Clinton administration: offer no "new polestar." This approach allowed Clinton to sustain his domestic mandate but it left the United States unprepared to deal with the threat posed by transnational terrorism and other post-Cold War security issues such as ethnic conflicts. With America engaged in two wars and a new phase in the war on terror set to begin (go after al Qaeda as Obama promised) an obvious question surfaces: US security suffered during the Clinton era because the former president failed to provide a new polestar; what price will the country pay this time?

THE POST COLD WAR NEMESIS: THE SEARCH FOR A POLESTAR

Since the collapse of the Soviet Union, marking the end to superpower ideological schism, the United States government and the foreign policy community commenced a new version of the Holy Grail: the search for a polestar, or if you will, a new framework to guide postwar US foreign policy. From the presidency of Harry S. Truman through the presidency of George Herbert Walker Bush American foreign policy was guided by the venerable Containment policy. Similarly, and a point often overlooked, Containment benefited from National Security Directive 68 (NSC-68) which assisted in preparing the national security bureaucracy and the American people for the long arduous struggle with Communism.

In the post-Cold War era, unlike the post-WW II period, the search for a new grand strategy has not been a successful one. A grand strategy is a construct that when implemented provides the guiding intellectual underpinning of US foreign policy. American grand strategy consists of four basic strategic formulations: isolationism or restraint, selective engagement, cooperative security, and primacy. These formulations appear simple enough, but a fundamental questions remains: After sixteen years why have three presidents failed to develop a grand strategy to replace containment, and what are the expectations that President Obama will be successful when all other previous post-Cold War presidents have failed?

In the wake of the collapse of the Soviet Union, President George H.W. Bush appeared shaken, often waiting for a clarification that validated the already certain international reaction that "The Cold War is over." In the midst of this psyche the Bush administration held firm to traditional Cold War beliefs and attitudes. The responses to the transforming historical events left the Bush administration unprepared to deal with the ethno-religious conflicts that dominated Central Europe and parts of Africa. Critics claimed that President Bush became a victim of the so-called "vision thing"; he failed to provide a new grand strategy that would end the extraordinarily brilliant life-cycle of containment. In the end Containment had an extended shelf life, continuing well into presidency of Bill Clinton.

Under President Clinton a new policy appeared to surface: Dual Containment. Historically speaking dual containment existed long before Clinton entered the White House. Both President Ronald Reagan and his successor George H.W. Bush employed an informal dual containment of Iran and Iraq. This statement requires a clarification. In the case of Reagan even though there was an attempt by the president to contain both Iraq and Iran, the policy was undermined by foolish efforts to engage both countries. Each effort proved problematic. With regard to Bush the prevailing view within the Clinton administration is that dual containment did not become an official policy of the President Bush until after the First Gulf War. From the opening months of the Clinton administration dual containment appeared to be the grand strategy of choice (it was not; dual containment was a regional strategy). The incessant military engagements with Iraq's Saddam Hussein and rhetoric by Clinton administration officials to Iran's theocracy on the need for engagement or Tehran would remain an international pariah state provided ample evidence of the president's policy to contain the dual regional threats to US and allied interests.

Long before the demise of dual containment, President Clinton unveiled the official administration grand strategy: Engagement and Enlargement. The details of the strategy were released in National Security Strategy of the White House in 1996. The document endeavored to provide a sense of optimism about the way forward:

> A new international era presents the United States with many distinct dangers, but also with a generally improved security environment and a range of opportunities to improve

it further. The preeminent threat that dominated our engagement during the Cold War has been replaced by a complex set of challenges. Our nation's strategy for defining and addressing those challenges has several core principles that guide our policies to safeguard American security, prosperity and fundamental values. First and foremost, we must exercise global leadership. We are not the world's policeman, but as the word's premier economic and military power, and with the strength of our democratic values, US engagement is indispensable to the forging of stable political relations and open trade to advance our interests.[76]

The critical passages of the document spelled out the objectives of enlargement and engagement. On enlargement Clinton's strategy was spelled out this way: "Our engagement must be selective, focusing on the challenges that are most important our own interests and focusing our resources where we can make the most difference. We must also use the right tools—being willing to act unilaterally when our direct national interests are most at stake; in alliance and partnership when our interests are shared by others; and multilaterally when our interests are more general and the problems are best addressed by the international community."[77] On engagement the document noted that this aspect of the strategy represented "A framework of democratic enlargement that increases our security by protecting, consolidating and enlarging the community of free market democracies. Our efforts focus on strengthening democratic processes in key emerging democratic states including Central and Eastern Europe, Russia, Ukraine and other new independent states of the former Soviet Union."[78]

President Clinton's strategy of enlargement and engagement was roundly criticized. According to Benjamin Schwarz the strategy failures were viewed this way: Clinton drifts "from crisis to crisis, never stepping back from the crush of events to design "structures," "frameworks," "overarching" concepts, and "architectures."[79] In a far more piquant analysis Robert Manning and Patrick Clawson observed "this is the administration that gave us "Engagement and Enlargement" as its national strategy. The term "engagement" is admirably intended to convey an embrace of internationalism and rejection of isolationism. But what it has meant in practice has tended to be a triumph of process over substance. And on the "engagement" they were equally expressive: "By "enlargement" the administration means expanding the community of democratic states. But the US role in promoting democracy, while important, is limited. Furthermore, it is not clear how important democracy is for national security strategy."[80]

The aforementioned criticisms were insightful. In the end critics charged that Clinton conducted foreign policy without a grand strategy, preferring "incrementalism" as a substitute for "grandness," a process that led to disaster. With regard to the issue of disaster, for example, while the document mentioned "combating terrorism" the Clinton administration never provided a coherent strategy to confront the singular threat to US security—transnational terrorism. This major strategic oversight, the consequence of inept strategic thinking, paved the way for the tragic events September 11, 2001.

President George W. Bush's grand strategy has been viewed through the prism of transformation. Transformation is verbiage used to impart a shift from the post-Cold War era to the post-September world. In any discourse on the grand strategy that evolved under President Bush the centerpiece of the new approach is found in the National Security Strategy of United States issued in 2002 and 2003. In 2002 The National Security Strategy asserted that "in an age where the enemies of civilization openly and actively seek the world's most destructive technologies, the United States cannot remain idle while dangers gather. We will always proceed deliberately, weighing the consequences of our actions."[81] In The National Security Strategy of 2003 the words preemption and prevention appeared prominently in the document. Preemption and prevention governed the threats posed by terrorists and rogue states. In time commentators began to call the new strategy the Bush Doctrine. Almost from the inception of the Bush Doctrine the threatened use of preemption and prevention induced a fire storm of criticism, most notably that it violated traditional American diplomatic traditions, and it would violate international norms regarding when a state could and could not use force. The doctrine indeed the strategy came under criticism in November of 2002 following the decision to use the Predator Unmanned Aerial Vehicle (UAV) to destroy six suspect Al Qaeda terrorists considered responsible for the October 17, 2000 attack on the USS Cole. The preventive war in Iraq induced a new round of criticism with many suggesting the action was a war of choice and hence a gross violation of international law.

In response to these criticism conservative commentators argued President Bush's critics dismissed two essential characteristics of the new strategy: that it provided moral clarity for US foreign policy and second it provided an approach that confronted America's enemies that threatened its interests. Another incantation of the Bush Doctrine had been advanced during the 2005 State of the Union Address, and again in The National Security Strategy 2006. Both had one thing in common: the advancement of democracy. On this point Joseph Nye had this say:

> Bush has increasingly emphasized the democratization component of his grand strategy. The 2006 National Security Strategy refers to democracy and freedom more than 200 times (three times as often as the 2002 document), downplays preventive war, and even includes a chapter on globalization (a subject Bush once privately derided as "mushy Clintonism"). The shift has been more than rhetorical: Bush's diplomacy toward North Korea and Iran has recently been much more multilateral than it was during his first term. Senior administration officials believe that Bush's aggressive democratization will prove successful and that the next president will be bound to follow the broad lines of Bush's new strategy. Vice President Dick Cheney expressed the administration's confidence in January, predicting that in a decade observers will "look back on this period of time and see that liberating 50 million people in Afghanistan and Iraq really did represent a major, fundamental shift, obviously, in US policy in terms of how we dealt with the emerging terrorist threat—and that we'll have fundamentally changed circumstances in that part of the world."[82]

The grand strategy approach adopted by President Bush in the wake of September 11, 2001 proved effective until the decision was made to invade Iraq. Thereafter critics openly criticized President Bush's grand strategy. In one example a critic of President Bush observed:

> America has been adrift for too long. The attacks of September 11th did not "change everything," but exacerbated the difficulty of articulating a purpose for American power since the Berlin Wall fell nearly two decades ago. America has suffered from strategic whiplash: the nebulousness of the post-Cold War era was rapidly replaced by a post-9/11 myopia on Islamist extremism and the so-called "war on terrorism." This myopia lay at the

root of the decision to invade Iraq in 2003, and it remains the chief obstacle preventing the emergence of a reasoned and pragmatic debate over the purpose of American power in the 21st century. The absence of a true grand strategy imperils America. The Bush administration has pursued a foreign policy that is narrow in its view, negative in its purpose, and has produced negligible results. Americans deserve a grand strategy that is panoramic in view, positive in its purpose, and persuasive as a basis for the continued exercise of American power.[83]

In the end though there are acceptable aspects of President Bush's grand strategy but it is not one that will survive during the administration of President Obama, who views the doctrine as the principal source of anti-Americanism and the mismanagement of US foreign policy. At issue, what are the prospects for a new and sustainable grand strategy under President Obama?

OBAMA AND GRAND STRATEGY

There is a near universal sentiment in the foreign policy community and the media: the need for President Barack Obama to develop an intellectual framework to guide his administrations stewardship of US foreign policy. A few statements exemplify the point. According to Fareed Zakaria, host of *CNN*'s GPS, he endeavored to warn President Obama that "any new attempt at a grand strategy for today must also begin with an accurate appraisal of the world." In his opinion "The Obama administration should study the National Intelligence Council's newly published forecast "Global Trends 2025: A Transformed World." The document provides significant evidence that identifies an international system that was constructed after World War II that will be dramatically altered by 2025. The cause of the transformation is the result of a burgeoning "transfer of global wealth and economic power now underway—roughly from West to East—is without precedent in modern history."[84] In the end, according to Zakaria, any new grand strategy that does not recognize these factors is doomed to failure. Zakaria makes this additional point, one that is critical to fashioning a workable, indeed a sustainable grand strategy: "Strategy begins by looking at the world and identifying America's interests, the threats to them and the resources available to be deployed. By relating all these, one can develop a set of foreign policies that will advance America's interests and ideals."[85]

Zakaria's perspective notwithstanding, there are many individuals that questioned whether President Obama is up to the task of creating a definable or measurable grand strategy. Often these critiques are posed in the following manner: "Obama claims to represent a paradigmatic shift in foreign policy thinking. He'll write a new chapter in American foreign policy. But what are his overarching strategic objectives? How do they differ from the Bush administration's stated goals which called for preserving American military supremacy worldwide and "precluding the rise of a great power rival?"[86]

Thomas Barnett asserts that any meaningful grand strategy can not and will not emerge, if it ever does, until President Obama sorts through the pros and cons of the residual effects of the Bush-Cheney years.

> Herein [is] the great opportunity of Obama's first term: stretching that wiggle space until there is real room for diplomatic maneuvering. Under Bush-Cheney, that space

was almost nonexistent for emerging and isolated powers, given the administration's twin demands that they combat transnational terrorism in the preferred manner while moving smartly toward democracy—somewhat contradictory goals not easily achieved in tandem during a frontier-integrating age full of real and virtual insurgencies. Over the next four years, Obama will spend most of his time and attention unwinding the twin negative legacies of Bush-Cheney: the two wars and the financial overhang. On the side, but somewhat in conjunction with that, he will seek to renegotiate America's relationship with the world—a global community that has bought into our baseline economic model (markets with various levels of state intervention) but still has a long way to go on top-line political achievement (democracy).[87]

According to Barnett President Obama's dilemma or opportunity, depending upon one's perspective, will depend on how he confronts the lingering impact of the Bush Doctrine which has been discredited in the wake if "the administration's shabby postwar efforts in both Iraq and Afghanistan that no successor is immediately required to clear the global palate."[88]

Speaking on the need to define an effective strategy to govern the war on terror, *Washington Post* columnist Eugene Robinson offered this warning to President Obama:

A concept that excludes nothing defines nothing. That's why one of the most urgent tasks for President-elect Barack Obama's "Team of Rivals" foreign policy brain trust is coming up with a coherent intellectual framework—and a winning battle plan—for the globe-spanning asymmetrical conflict that George W. Bush calls the "war on terror."[89]

Many assert that an appropriate framework is the one "sweeping Washington," one used incessantly by Secretary of Defense Robert Gates who employs the phrase "full spectrum operations" to describe 'multidisciplinary security and development campaigns?'"[90] David Brooks provides a more detailed assessment of the important new *lingua franca* in foreign policy:

Gates has told West Point cadets that more regime change is unlikely but that they may spend parts of their careers training soldiers in allied nations. He has called for more spending on the State Department, foreign aid and a revitalized US Information Agency. He's spawned a flow of think-tank reports on how to marry hard and soft preemption. The Bush administration began to implement these ideas, but in small and symbolic ways. President Bush called for a civilian corps to do nation-building. National Security Presidential Directive 44 laid out a framework so different agencies could coordinate foreign reconstruction and stabilization. The Millennium Challenge Account program created a method for measuring effective governance. Actual progress was slow, but the ideas developed during the second Bush term have taken hold. Given the events of the past years, the US is not about to begin another explicit crusade to spread democracy. But decent effective and responsive government would be a start. Obama and his team didn't invent this approach. But if they can put it into action that would be continuity we can believe in.[91]

There is a small and growing minority that observes that there are a number of constraints that will impact President Obama's efforts to construct a post-Bush strategy framework: "Obama will face pressure to develop a grand strategy within the constraints of a global financial crisis that is likely to crunch US discretionary spending, much of which is dedicated to defense. He will have to prioritize funds for troops, equipment, and diplomatic missions: a task that may ultimately lead to cuts in major weapon programs."[92]

Other commentators had an altogether dissimilar message. The warning, simply stated, was to avoid wasting time and energy on a grand strategy. Such a view is consistent with the thinking of Ralph Peters who added this warning:

> My Advice to President-Elect Obama: Don't do it! Don't listen to the desk-bound academics and pundits who want you to develop a "new grand strategy" for our foreign policy. The answer for the US isn't to "think globally and act locally" but to "think locally and act globally".... Political and strategic "unified-field theories" don't just kill they kill for no good purpose. Rather than attempting to impose a new grand strategy on the world, our government must formulate *regional* strategies that contain within them country-specific strategies-recognizing that Brazil isn't identical to Bolivia and that Iran's challenges are profoundly different from those of its next-door neighbor, Afghanistan.[93]

Accepting the advice of Peters could prove disastrous for Obama, but tragically if history is our guide, he may indeed follow the caveats laid out in the aforementioned excerpt. In the end, however, it is not the advice of Peters that Obama will follow but the approach employed by President Clinton.

What are the arguments to validate the contention that Obama is more likely to adopt the Clinton approach, namely avoid a grand strategy altogether? Before answering this question it is appropriate to return to Clinton and his efforts to end the search for a polestar. To be clear Clinton's proposal and later the implementation of the strategy of enlargement and engagement was never viewed as a serious replacement for containment. The obvious question on the minds of many would be this: What accounts for so many within the foreign policy community who were so dismissive of Clinton's grand strategy selection? The answer is the strategy never addressed existing threats to US interests that developed during the Clinton era, nor did it identify those threats that would emerge in the future. Specifically the strategy based on "selective engagement" appeared more concerned with threats to "the community of democratic states" and less on the question of terrorism where the strategy proved vacuous. In the end most assert that the document, in its entirety, had merits but there is another group of scholars that argued that any criticism the Clinton administration deserves with regard to a grand strategy is in the area of "execution rather than principles. The administration has been short-sighted and naive, not soft or isolationist. Yet engaging does not equal acting strategically, and a willingness to use military force does not equate with using force effectively."[94]

The reality is that Clinton had a grand strategy in name only. The document failed to define the mission of the United States in the post-Cold War world. It did define and clarify the interests of the country, but the scope was viewed to be too narrow and the response to most threats unfocused. To identify why Clinton's strategy was a colossal failure, it is important to keep in mind that, as is the case with containment, a successful grand strategy is durable and could possibly shape US foreign policy for decades. In the end Clinton's grand strategy is one of restraint. In the final analysis for many in the foreign policy community Clinton's grand strategy impressed few and its shelf life was deemed insufficient.

There is an underlying finality that symbolizes Clinton's grand strategy: its intended purpose was to serve as a mirage for a strategy that wasn't. That is President Clinton wanted nothing on the foreign policy front to interfere with his electoral mandate, which called for fixing the economy. Indeed with the Cold War over and the "peace dividend" in full swing it was the president's natural inclination to prioritize domestic issues over those on the foreign policy front. Thus the prevailing view among the president's political advisors was to keep foreign policy from interfering with the domestic agenda. The strategy of enlargement and engagement contributed to this philosophy by ensuring that Clinton's view of the world would be unfocused and there be no mention of a central threat. If such a threat existed a major increase in defense expenditures could endanger the president's efforts to balance the national budget. There would be consequences for the diversion. The two preeminent consequences came in the form of Al Qaeda, who's networked flourished and attacked US interests with impunity, and second, proliferation expanded to India and Pakistan, as a result of black market network led by A. Q. Khan which provided technology and components to Libya, North Korea and Iran. In the view of the logic of many members of the Clinton administration confronting al Qaeda in Afghanistan could derail presidential focus on the economy.

In the case of President Obama there are indeed some parallels with Clinton. Both were dedicated to curing the ailing American economy. There is little doubt that what confronts Obama far exceeds the situation encountered by Clinton. That said like Clinton expect that Obama's grand strategy will be one of selective engagement and one governed by restraint. This perspective is hardly farfetched. In the words of Barry Posen the next grand strategy is one that is likely to "conceive [of] its security interests narrowly, use its military power stingily, pursue its enemies quietly but persistently, share responsibilities and costs more equitably, watch and wait more patiently. Let's do this for 16 years and see if the outcomes aren't better."[95]

A strategy of selective engagement, as was the case with Clinton, would be perfect for President Obama. It would provide domestic cover for implementing Obama's campaign strategy for withdrawing US troops from Iraq. Consistent with Clinton, there is little demand for a grand strategy. First, despite the need for a grand strategy, it is still a province of foreign policy elites; a group that lacks the ability and resources to make the noise to draw in the American people. Second, there is no demand for one. Again, there should be a demand but the reality is post-Modern presidents (Clinton, Bush, and now Obama) have a major advantage over previous presidents. Traditional and Modern presidents had to confront threats from states. The threats and the violence from these states were far more consistent and the lives lost are on a scale for higher than attacks conducted by today's threats which are largely non-state or transnational.

The aforementioned reality permitted Clinton, and now President Obama, to provide a grand strategy that will in no way end the search for a strategic framework to supplant containment. Under Obama expect not only a selective engagement approach, but one that will be incremental and one that places Obama in a position where he is incessantly reacting to crisis after crisis. It would be far more beneficial to President Obama and for US foreign policy to have a cohesive grand strategy that is proactive. The latter would prove counterproductive for Obama. Consistent with Clinton, Obama wants freedom action to deal with an ailing economy that is in the throws of an extended recession. Thus a grand strategy that details not only the interests of the United States but how the Obama administration would respond to those threats would force the president, when those interests are attacked, to use military force.

President Obama's grand strategy will have the following components: Terrorism, Proliferation, Global Warming and Resource Politics. Obama's strategy is likely to be governed by "incrementalism and push a new international social contract between the US and the rest of the world."[96] Beyond this Obama is unlikely to provide a strategic replacement for containment. This is the case because among Obama's core advisors no intellectual strategic thinker exists within the administration. This is a problem that plagued the Bush administration, and certainly the Clinton administration. Obama is now the fourth US president given the task of redefining American grand strategy. What is likely is that when the Obama administration concludes the search for a polestar will commence again. History indicates the absence of a grand strategy will increase threats to US interests. Similarly the president is incessantly shifting from one crisis to next, a process that has proven disastrous to American national security.

CHAPTER 4
CONFRONTING THE HINGE POWERS

The Obama presidency, much like the Bush and Clinton presidencies, will be devoid of a global challenge from any state. That said Obama will have to contend with a dizzying array of "hinge powers"—emerging powers that pose disparate threats to US regional interests—that are showing signs of flexing their muscles. States such as China (economic and a potential military threat), Russia (political and potential military threat), Japan and India (both in the economic realm) are certain to challenge the United States in one form or another. Several examples are instructive. One day after Obama's electoral victory Russian President Dmitri Medvedev threatened to install Iskander intermediate range missiles on the borders of Poland should the US move forward with deployment of the missile defense shield. The Chinese threat may involve the Taiwan question which remains an explosive issue that could emerge as a test of Obama's resolve. There is another threat, but it is one on paper and one unlikely to materialize: The European Union. The European Union (EU) is another hinge threat, but one which should be filed under the words "paper challenge." In reality the potential does exist for a "triple challenge"—economic, political and military—but such power in terms of global threat is a fantasy. Instead the EU threat is one that is more likely to appear in the political realm, where member states, rather than the collective organization, will from time to time protest US policies around the world. That said the most likely challenges may come from three states, India, Russia, and China. The dilemmas posed by the aforementioned hinge powers, and how Obama manages them, are the focus of this chapter.

OBAMA AND INDIA

As a candidate Obama captured the attention of Indian Americans and the people of India after he made two significant statements. In the first statement he spoke of the significance of India's beloved hero Mahatma Gandhi and how he impacted his life. According to Obama, "In my life, I have always looked to Mahatma Gandhi as an inspiration, because he embodied the kind of transformational change that can be made when ordinary people come together to do extraordinary things. That is why his (Gandhi's) portrait hangs in my Senate office; to remind me that real results will not just come from Washington, they will come from the people."[97]

The second statement is equally important, particularly when he identified India as significance priority in his foreign policy agenda. In the words of Obama, "The US should be <u>working</u> with India on a range of critical issues, from preventing terrorism to promoting peace and stability in Asia. Mr. Joe Biden and I will make building a stronger relationship, including a close strategic partnership, with India a top priority."[98]

Obama promised to make "India a top priority." This is a bold statement; one would suspect that President Obama would provide specifics as to how he would improve upon the policies developed during the last two years of the Bush administration. Since the presidential campaign has yet to disclose his administrations policy toward India. In his last statement on India, in an interview with IANS, then Senator Obama in October 2008 made the following comment: "I also believe India is a natural strategic partner for America in the 21st century and that the US should be working with India" a host of significant issues that impact both countries in the region. Second, in the same interview Obama stated there are additional issues in the relationship that are significant. Those issues range from comprehensive immigration reforms and making "globalization and trade work for American workers, to seeking the active participation of the Indian American community in the process of change that he has advocated." Obama went on to make supplemental comments. The Obama administration, he said, would seek to strengthen ties with the "vibrant" Indian American community and encourage their "active engagement... in making the change we seek."[99]

A critical area issue in the Indo-US relationship concerns the contentious issue of Indian nuclear weapons and the Nuclear Proliferation Treaty (NPT). On the latter Obama said nothing. On the former, in the same interview he was asked to address this question:

"You have voted for the Indo-US nuclear deal. Would you consider India a strategic partner with the United States in its efforts to promote stability in the Asian region?" Obama responded to the question this way: "I am an advocate of strengthening US relations with India, the world's largest democracy and a growing economic power. I voted for the India civilian nuclear cooperation deal in 2006 and have since worked to ensure that the agreement is implemented properly so that Indians benefit from expanded energy sources and that nuclear proliferation concerns are addressed."[100]

The proliferation question is controversial by itself, but Obama weighed-in on an issue that is at the heart of Indo-Pak dispute: the future of Kashmir. During the course of interview on *MSNBC* on November 2, 2008 Obama urged India to resolve the issue over the disputed territory of Kashmir. According to Obama with this issue no longer the center of gravity of Indo-Pak relations, Pakistan could turn its attention toward increased cooperation to end the Taliban insurgency. Obama issued this statement during the *MSNBC* interview: "The most important thing we're going to have to do with respect to Afghanistan is actually deal with Pakistan. And we've got to work with the newly elected government there (Pakistan) in a coherent way that says, terrorism is now a threat to you. Extremism is a threat to you. We should—try to resolve the Kashmir crisis so that they (Pakistan) can stay focused not on India, but on the situation with those militants."[101]

The statement was viewed very positively in India; indeed some used verbiage like "Obama Thesis" to describe his comments. According to C. Raja Mohan, the thesis is succinct: "The sources of Afghan instability are in Pakistan; those in turn are linked to Islamabad's conflict with New Delhi, at the heart of which is Jammu and Kashmir."[102] What appeared like a genuine opening became a source of controversy for Obama. First, among his advisors it appeared that he "went over the cliff," a reference that he was too specific, and that India views the Kashmir dispute as a matter of its internal affairs, and has historically precluded outside mediation over the controversial issue. Second, conservatives argued that Obama's position on Kashmir could backfire. According to Lisa Curtis and Walter Lohman, in Heritage Foundation Special Report, titled "Stiffening Pakistan's Resolve Against Terrorism: A Memo to President-elect Obama," acknowledged that "by raising unrealistic expectations for a favorable settlement among Pakistanis, thereby fuelling Islamabad's support for militants in hopes of pushing a hard-line agenda," and that "Your recent assertion that the US should try to help resolve the Kashmir issue so that Pakistan can focus on reining in militancy on its Afghan border is misguided."[103]

As the world's most populous democracy India's threat to the United States is confined to the economic realm. Like China, India has had extraordinary growth rates since the turn of century.[104] While India is a hinge power one should not to see this growth as threatening but rather a challenge. If the US economic strength continues to decline, then India may be considered a threat. This statement is validated by Eswar Prasad who observed the Indo-US relationship can be categorized as a vibrant economic partnership.[105] Prasad does acknowledge there are areas of concern. He asserts "India poses challenges in areas ranging from integrating global agricultural markets to combating climate change, and the country's success in global high value services markets has complicated America's internal debate on trade. America must look for areas of cooperation where possible and deepen bilateral engagement broadly in order to make progress on its agenda."[106]

There are additional areas of concern for Indo-US relations. One area of concern is in the high technology sector. According to Intel Chairman Andrew S. Grove (a concern no doubt shared by his successors Craig Barrett and Paul Otellini) by 2010 India is positioned to supplant the United States in software and tech-service jobs. What is behind India's challenge? As one would anticipate "The nation's software and service businesses are under siege by countries like India and China taking advantage of cheap labor costs and strong incentives for new financial investment."[107] The impact, according to the Forrester Research, is that the result of this challenge posed by India could cost US companies in the combined industries up to 3.3 million jobs by 2015.

A second area of concern is economic, but it does have political implications. Resource politics is at the heart of the challenge not just to the American economy, but to US foreign policy. It is important to note that China and India are involved in this challenge:

> Chinese and Indian investments in countries and regions of US concern include India's multibillion dollar project to pipe in Iranian gas via Pakistan, a plan criticized … by US Secretary of State Condoleezza Rice; billion-dollar investments by India's main oil and gas enterprise in far-flung projects that include Syria-accused by Washington of failing to prevent insurgents from crossing its border into Iraq and of suppressing democracy in Lebanon. India has also signed a pipeline deal with gas-rich Myanmar's hard-line military junta.[108]

The high tech (software and tech-service jobs) and the resource challenge collectively illustrate the continuing shift of global influence from the West to the East. Indeed this conspicous challenge—primarily as the result of the global financial crisis—may end the notion of a second "American Century." There is another view that is taking center stage. That is according to Fareed

Zakaria what is occurring is not so much a prediction of the decline of the United States, but the fact that the rest of the world is assuming its natural place in the post-Cold War and post-September 11 Worlds.[109]

The aforementioned issues are indicative of the Indian challenge. It is critical that President Obama address these and other issues. Though the threats are by no means imminent or in the category of the "threats" posed by Russia and China, they are nonetheless issues that are formidable challenges. Suggests to the president to confronting the Indian challenge are as follows:

Step One: President Obama has to strengthen the American economy, particularly in the area of the budget deficit. A robust American economy can be used as a tool to defuse any short term and possible long term economic challenge by India. Consistent with this point, President Obama should follow some aspects of Bush administration policy.

Step Two: The Bush administration made a major decision: in recognition of India's continuing economic power status the US government accepted that rise and actively sought economic partnerships. The Obama administration can easily build on what has been started under the Bush administration. Here are some areas for future economic partnerships. There are six priority areas that include the following: (1) Promotion of Trade and Industry; here both states can partner "to make the Doha Round of the WTO a success by showing leadership to support an ambitious outcome and making strong offers in all the key areas of negotiations"; (2) Creation of an Infrastructure Development Fund: "This could act as a vehicle for US investment into Indian infrastructure"; (3) Promote Technology Exchange in Agriculture, Biotechnology and Nanotechnology: "through a combination of exchange of scientists between Universities/Labs in the two countries and by setting up Centers for R&D in these fields supported by the two Governments"; (4) Partner in Skills Development: US and Indian companies could work together for joint sponsorship of select Industrial Training Institutes (ITIs) in India and/or in the setting up of new institutes"; (5) Set up an Indo-US Center for Industrial R&D "in product design and development—with support from U.S and Indian industry and government"; and (6) Establish a Dispute Resolution Mechanism: "A dispute settlement mechanism that has the power and jurisdiction to resolve commercial and contractual disputes quickly could be set up by India."[110]

Step Three: The continuing partnerships may not end the Indian challenge, but they will ensure that India will never rise to threaten American primacy over the global economy. In another area that has more to do with campaign promises and domestic political clamor, there is no doubt that Obama will bring up the issue of "outsourcing." This will no doubt be an issue of contention in future Indo-US discussions, but one should not aspect any significant change with regard to the issue of outsourcing. In other words, the loss of jobs is important, but Obama will have to weigh this issue with India's role in the war on terror, managing Indo-Pak relations, and dealing with the Indian economic rise.

Step Four: In the wake of the Mumbai terrorist attack experts recognized that there was a homegrown Pakistani component. The Bush administration used private diplomacy to ensure that the domestic clamor for revenge among the Indian population was not acted upon. There is little doubt the US government feared a counter strike but worked to defuse any potential political-military crisis. The Obama administration can learn much from the Bush administration's actions, most notably the preventive diplomacy that forestalled two mini crises, one in 2001 (when Indian members of parliament were killed by terrorists from Pakistan) and another in the wake of the fallout from the recent Mumbai terrorist attack. Similarly, the actions of President Bush preserved the burgeoning economic relationship. At issue, what actions will President Obama take in the event of a subsequent crisis to preserve the on-going economic and burgeoning strategic relationship?

OBAMA AND RUSSIA

The Russian threat to the United States is one that has raised concerns in the Pentagon and the State Department. The Russian hinge threat is compromised of political and military dimensions. In November of 2008 the US Senate Select Committee on Intelligence held its annual hearings on national security issues. Appearing before the committee Michael McConnell, President Bush's National Intelligence Director, discussed the potential threats posed by Al Qaeda and Iran. McConnell's comments on the aforementioned threats were consistent with previous threat assessments: each posed short term and long term threats to US security.

On Russia McConnell noted there are a range of threats and that "Each of them is quite serious, and I wouldn't select any of them as the top one." According to McConnell the threats consist of the modernization of the Russian Army; Russian supplies of fuel to Iran to advance their nuclear program; the burgeoning cyber threat; the overall modernization of its military, particularly in the Naval surface fleets, and then he listed another threat that many overlook: Russian efforts to use its energy resources as a political weapon. He made this additional comment, "Aggressive Russian efforts to control, restrict or block the transit of hydrocarbons from the Caspian to the West—and to ensure that East-West energy corridors remain subject to Russian control—underscore the potential power and influence of Russia's energy policy."[111] Collectively, the overall threat is anticipated to "expand over the next four years."[112]

During the presidential election Obama conveyed little about how he would deal with the always complex US-Russian relationship. In an address to the Chicago Council on Global Affairs on April 23, 2007 Obama made the following statement about the Russia threat, "We know that Russia is neither our enemy nor close ally right now, and we shouldn't shy away from pushing for more democracy, transparency, and accountability in that country."[113]

There are a number of issues that have strained the US-Russian relationship, whether in the form of criticism of the Russian government's anti-democratic practices, to the placement of a US missile defense in former communist satellite countries, and NATO expansion, or Russia's use of Venezuelan bases for its Backfire Bomber are just few points of contention. During the presidential campaign and also during the early months of his presidency Obama did not mention any of these issues. Instead during the campaign Obama made the decision to explore an issue that could be used for cooperation. The issue was nonproliferation. On this point Obama was succinct: "The nonproliferation regime is being challenged, and new civilian nuclear programs could spread the means to make nuclear weapons." And when he became president Obama observed "I will work with other nations to secure, destroy, and stop the spread of these weapons in order to dramatically reduce the nuclear dangers for our nation and the world. America must lead a global effort to secure all nuclear weapons and material at vulnerable sites within four years—the most effective way to prevent terrorists from acquiring a bomb." Obama conceded that Russian cooperation is essential to his efforts to halt the spread of nuclear weapons: "This will require the active cooperation of Russia. Although we must not shy away from pushing for more democracy and accountability in Russia, we must work with the country in areas of common interest—above all, in making sure that nuclear weapons and material are secure. We must also work with Russia to update and scale back our dangerously outdated Cold War nuclear postures and de-emphasize the role of nuclear weapons. America must not rush to produce a new generation of nuclear warheads. And we should take advantage of recent technological advances to build bipartisan consensus behind ratification of the Comprehensive Test Ban Treaty. All of this can be done while maintaining a strong nuclear deterrent. These steps will ultimately strengthen, not weaken, our security."[114]

Other than these two statements, the next time Obama would make a statement of consequence about Russia came in the wake of Moscow's invasion of Georgia. By all accounts Obama's comments were nuanced, and he was criticized for not displaying more resolve.

Interestingly in the wake of Obama's historic electoral victory, the focus on Russia increased. Russian President Dmitry Medvedev's congratulatory message to Barack Obama on his electoral victory provided the opening salvo for discourse on US-Russian relations. The bulk of his message was indeed conciliatory: "Russian-American relations have historically been an important factor for stability in the world and have great importance and sometimes key significance for resolving many of today's international and regional problems. We in Russia are certain of the need to work consistently on developing cooperation between our countries not only on the broad range of issues in the international agenda but also on building real bilateral cooperation in all different areas. We have already built up solid positive potential in this area but much still remains to be done for the good of our peoples and in the interests of making the world more peaceful and secure. I hope for a constructive dialogue with you based on trust and consideration of each other's interests."[115]

Medvedev's conciliatory comments received scant press attention; rather the Russian president's threat the morning after Obama's election victory garnered the most media coverage. The threat included the following: Medvedev threatened to install Iskander intermediate range missiles on the borders of Poland should the US move forward with deployment of the missile defense shield; second Medvedev acknowledged the missiles would be deployed "to neutralize if necessary the anti-ballistic missile system in Europe," and finally the Russian president promised to deploy its Navy off Kaliningrad and to install electronic jamming devices to disrupt the US shield that relies on a radar station in the Czech Republic and ten interceptor missiles in Poland. These actions according to the Russian president are mechanisms that "must be created to block mistaken, egotistical and sometimes simply dangerous decisions of certain members of the international community."[116] The "certain members" mentioned in the above quote are a reference to actions the Russian government perceives as a new effort of encirclement of his country. There was no response by President Bush or Obama to statements made by Medvedev.

With the presidential campaign over, Obama used the transition period to make statements about the US-Russian relationship. On the *NBC* program "Meet the Press" Obama stressed that "I think that it's going to be important for us *to reset* US-Russia relations. And when it comes to Georgia and their threats against their neighboring countries, I think they've been acting in ways that are contrary to international norms.

We want to cooperate with them where we can, but we … also have to send a clear message that they have to act in ways that are not bullying their neighbors."[117]

Once in office President Obama and his foreign policy team commenced the always bureaucratic "review" of US policy toward Russia. In confronting the Russian threat there are some obvious realities that any US president will have to confront. Obama, during a debate with

Senator McCain, provided a statement that indicated that he was aware of the dangers posed by Russia: "A resurgent and very aggressive Russia is a threat to the peace and stability of the region."[118]

Irrespective of the ongoing review of US-Russia relations President Obama has settled on a short term policy: resetting US relations with Russia. Evidence of the policy emerged in two forms. The first time occurred during Vice President Joseph Biden's visit to Munich, Germany at the Conference on Security Policy on February 7, 2009. During the visit Biden made the following comment: "It is time to press the reset button and to revisit the many areas where we can and should be working together with Russia."[119]

The second occasion regarding the establishment of the new relationship occurred during a meeting between Secretary of State Hillary Clinton and Russian Foreign Minister Sergey Lavrov in Geneva, Switzerland in March of 2009. During the press conference a confident and smiling Clinton remarked, "I would like to present you with a little gift that represents what President Obama and Vice President Biden and I have been saying and that is: 'We want to reset our relationship and so we will do it together.'" Presenting a button with the word *peregruzka,* what the US diplomats thought represented the Russian word for reset. Clinton added, "We worked hard to get the right Russian word. Do you think we got it?" In his answer Lavrov noted "You got it wrong. "It should be *perezagruzka* (the Russian word for reset).This says *peregruzka* which means overcharged."[120] Both Lavrov and Clinton laughed, but domestically and internationally the press had a field day. The press perspective is that after spending considerable time during the presidential campaign and during the opening months of the Obama presidency on devising a policy around the words "reset" one would think the new administration would know the Russian translation of the very word it identified symbolized as its policy.

The use of the word reset may be symbolic of President Obama's policy toward Russia, but in the view of many it is not a sound policy. Similarly, it does not really address some of the critical issues that have caused tensions between the two countries. Here are a few steps that should be taken to revitalize the relationship between the US and Russia.

Step One: In the final months of the Bush administration Obama's predecessor opened dialogue with the Russian government. During these negotiations President Bush offered "several new proposals to the Russians." The first called for allowing "Russian military officials to inspect the new installations planned in Poland and the Czech Republic for the new missile defense system." Similarly, there is another opportunity that is linked to the "Bush initiative": President Obama may want to "delay deployment of a missile shield in Poland until an Iranian nuclear threat—which Washington says is its reason for existing—has actually materialized, instead of doing so immediately."[121] With the element of time and the opportunities afforded by direct talks, this may offer Obama an opportunity to reduce US-Russian tensions.

Step Two: In another option Obama should try to build confidence building measures that could provide a mechanism to set the stage for a more productive relationship. The initial carrot "could come in the form of negotiating agreements with Russia." An obvious example would be pushing Russian "entry into the World Trade Organization and working with Moscow toward a way out of the missile defense morass." This diplomatic engagement would serve two purposes: alert NATO countries and the international community that efforts were made on the diplomatic front to seek a more productive relationship with Russia. Second, should this initiative fail then Obama could warn the Russians that his administration has offered avenues to pave the way for a productive relationship, but unless there are concessions or conciliatory gestures on the part of

Moscow, should the relationship continue on its negative path that they would be responsible for any "future US actions."

Step Three: Notwithstanding evidence of "cold war-type rhetoric" between the United States and Russia, prior to and in the wake of the Russian invasion of Georgia, there are areas where the US and the Russians have worked well together. Those areas involve the war on terror and the six party talks to contain and eliminate North Korean nuclear weapons. President Obama should work to affirm these important aspects of the relationship.

Step Four: There is a strong possibility that Russia may test Obama in the Ukraine or in the Czech Republic. If one of these realities should unfold, whether in the case of the aforementioned two States, or others in Central Europe, there is one thing President Obama cannot do: Obama can not "cede the former Soviet republics and satellites in Eastern Europe back into the orbit of what the Russians like to call their near abroad."[122] Similarly, should this scenario, or one like it comes to pass, Obama will have to avoid responses like those made immediately after the Russian invasion of Georgia. That is he must be decisive and his response should be multi-faceted.

Step Five: There are areas that could be used to reduce tensions. Those areas include US-Russian cooperation on the Israeli-Palestinian conflict; press for increased Russian involvement to divert Iran's nuclear ambitions, and given the current US-Russian nuclear agreement is set to expire, there is little doubt the Russians do not want to enter into a nuclear arms race with the United States. There is no doubt the Russian government understands this not a race they could win.[123] That said the recent Russian threat to modernize its military will prove interesting in the long term.

Step Six: There will be an opportunity for President Obama to meet with Medvedev. His senior foreign policy advisors will have to work to assure that Obama avoids a President John F. Kennedy moment, a reference to the fact that at the Vienna Summit the Secretary General of Soviet Communist Nikita Khrushchev perceived the American president as weak. This unfortunate perception paved the way for the Cuban missile crisis. While no crisis of this magnitude is likely in the Obama administration, the point herein is that "any misperception" of the US president may produce Russian adventurism.

These are critical steps to reducing US-Russian tensions in the short term. In the long term the Obama administration will have to work assiduously for a long term strategy that ends the acrimony that dominated the last two years of the Bush administration. This will be a critical test of Obama's new diplomacy.

OBAMA AND CHINA

During the presidential campaign Senator Obama opined about the threat posed by China. According to Obama, "China's rise offers great opportunity, but also poses serious challenges. It is critical the US do all it can to assure China's rise is peaceful, and, if it remains so, the US should welcome China's continuing emergence and prosperity."[124] On the issue of China Obama's foreign policy advisors did an exceptional job in "schooling" their candidate on the complex relationship with Beijing. Regardless of the venue, Obama made statements that indicated he would, in most areas, work to preserve the status quo.

On the always controversial Taiwan question, Obama made the following comment: "The US should be firm on issues that divide us like Taiwan while flexible on issues that could unite us."[125] What Obama's was apparently conveying is that if elected president he would not seek to transform and challenge the long-standing one-China policy. Obama's foreign policy surrogates Gregory B. Craig and Wendy R. Sherman, both former Clinton advisors, observed that not only are relations with China essential, but once elected Obama would make efforts to improve relations but should impress upon the leaders of China that in the area of trade they should anticipate change.

The following exchange during the *Des Moines Register* Democratic debate on December 13, 2007 provides a sense of Obama's views on Sino-American trade relations. During the debate Obama received the following question: "Given China's size, its muscular manufacturing capabilities, its military buildup, at this point—and also including its large trade deficit—at this point, who has more leverage, China or the US? Obama offered this response: "Number one is we've got to get our own fiscal house in order. Number two, when I was visiting Africa, I was told by a group of businessmen that the presence of China is only exceeded by the absence of America in the entire African continent. Number three, we have to be tougher negotiators with China. They are not enemies, but they are competitors of ours. Right now the United States is still the dominant superpower in the world. But the next president can't be thinking about today; he or she also has to be thinking about 10 years from now, 20 years from now, 50 years from now."[126]

Obama offered this declaratory response that was far more specific in how he would confront US-China trade relations. To ameliorate trade Obama suggests, "We should insist on labor standards and human rights, the opening of Chinese markets fully to American goods, and the fulfillment of legal contracts with American businesses but without triggering a trade war as prolonged instability in the Chinese economy could have global economic consequences."[127]

In another critical area of US-China relations, Obama contends that a major problem regarding declining American business competitiveness concerns China's ongoing currency manipulation that repeatedly undercuts US exports. Similarly, Obama observes that China continues to enforce US copyright and trademark laws, and the government in Beijing creates expansive "regulatory laws and tax barriers delivery and sale of technology goods and services abroad."[128] These issues, and others, Obama claims are actions that China engaged in and the Bush administration ignored.

Not long after his election President Obama received the traditional message of goodwill from a foreign leader. In keeping with this tradition President Hu Jintao of China sent him a congratulatory message. In the message Hu issued this statement to Obama: "China and the United States share broad common interests and important responsibilities on a wide range of major issues concerning the well-being of humanity. To grow long term healthy and stable China-US relations serves the fundamental interests of our countries and peoples and is of great significance to the maintenance and promotion of peace, stability and development in the world."[129]

With the traditions and the exchange of pleasantries over, the critical question for President Obama is how will he contend with the threat posed by China? As a hinge power, China's potential threat is an evolving one. David C. Hendrickson provides a sense of the Chinese threat.

> Over the next two decades China would achieve capabilities that would enable it to threaten war against the United States outside its near abroad or to stand in relation to the United States as the Soviet Union once did. The Taiwan question remains potentially explosive and could again become "the most dangerous spot on the planet," but it is

difficult to see any other Sino-American dispute reaching a flammable point. The United States will continue to enjoy escalation dominance but may lose military parity in the immediate theater (across the Taiwan Strait) as China builds its armed forces. China knows it would be madness to fight a war with the United States but has made it clear that Taiwanese independence is a red line, and it may be that Chinese popular opinion is even more hawkish on this question than is the Chinese state. In the longer run, it is evident that the management of China's rise by the United States (or shall we say the management of the incoherent American hyperpower by China?) is a political and military problem of the first order, and equally evident that historical precedents do not suggest a smooth adjustment.[130]

The political threat posed by China is an obvious one. In an effort to end genocide in Sudan the UN Security Council has attempted to introduce stringent sanctions against the Omar Bashir-led government, but repeatedly China has vetoed many of those efforts. China's national interest comes in the form of protecting its oil contracts with the Sudanese government. Elsewhere in Asia, the region is well aware of Beijing's economic influence, and China continues to establish trade agreements with many Asia-Pacific Economic Cooperation (APEC) countries that undermine US influence in the region. The Bush administration not only recognized this reality, but found it difficult to reverse the trend. Its failure to do more had to with the fact that the Bush administration needed China's influence in the US-led six party talks to contain North Korea's nuclear ambitions. In the end China's political influence in the region and elsewhere is a double-edged sword: Beijing is helpful in containing Kim's nuclear ambitions, and its influence is needed in the war on terror. However, on the question of genocide in Dardur, Sudan, along with the burgeoning economic influence in Asia, that political influence is considered an annoyance.

The military threat is an altogether different matter. The scope of China's military threat is open for debate. The Department of Defense 2006 Quadrennial Defense Review Report asserts "The People's Liberation Army (PLA) is in the process of long term transformation from a mass army designed for protracted wars of attrition on its territory to a more modern force capable of fighting short duration, high intensity conflicts against high-tech adversaries." Today, China's ability to sustain military power at a distance is limited. The report makes this statement: "China has the greatest potential to compete militarily with the United States and field disruptive military technologies that could over time offset traditional US military advantages."[131] The report suggests that in the near term "China's military build-up appears focused on preparing for Taiwan Strait contingencies, including the possibility of US intervention. However, analysis of China's military acquisitions suggests it is also generating capabilities that could apply to other regional contingencies, such as conflicts over resources or territory."[132]

The Pentagon is concerned about two additional issues: China's efforts to displace US military influence in Asia and the concern about a Chinese-led attack on Japan. With respect to the issue of displacement, Ted Galen Carpenter, the vice president for defense and foreign policy studies at the Cato Institute concluded: "The Pentagon believes the Chinese modernization is designed to create a dominant position in East Asia and displace the United States. That might be a long term goal, but you would have to measure that in decades, not years." On the Chinese threat to Japan, James Mulvenon, deputy director of the Center for Intelligence Research and Analysis, an independent research firm in Washington, argued "They are very worried the Chinese are posturing for a maritime confrontation with Japan."[133]

The recent March 2009 Annual Report On China's Military concluded that the US is concerned China was "developing weapons that would disable its enemies' space technology such as satellites, boosting its electromagnetic warfare and cyber-warfare capabilities and continuing to modernize its nuclear arsenal." Similarly, the Pentagon expressed concern about the "uncertainty [that] surrounds China's future course, particularly regarding how its expanding military power might be used."[134] The Chinese government's reaction was predictable: the report represented a "gross distortion of the facts" and it was product of "Cold War thinking."[135]

Critics of the aforementioned Pentagon's assessment argued that it is highly politicized and it is considered an effort designed to seek or to maintain current military expenditures.

The Council on Foreign Relations offered a dissimilar assessment. For example, while China is indeed increasing their military expenditures, it is too early to determine whether this translates into an immediate military threat. In another example, according to Richard C. Bush III, director of the Center for Northeast Asian Policy Studies at the Brookings Institution, "I believe China has not made the strategic choice of whether it should challenge the United States for dominance in Asia."[136] Similarly, the view among many experts is that China's military expansion is aimed at deterring a US military response to a crisis in the Taiwan Straits, a lesson learned from the incident in the straits during the Clinton administration.

In the end Hendrickson observes "Given the compelling interests of both sides in the avoidance of war, it should not be beyond the wit of statesmen to manage peacefully this power transition, but war cannot be excluded over the next several decades."[137] Thus in the final analysis the issue remains: what actions can the Obama administration take to avoid war? There are a number of options open to President Obama in dealing with the Chinese challenge. The options include the following:

Step One: President Obama may wish to continue the policy pursued by the last three US presidents which calls for a policy of engagement. Many opponents dislike the circumstances surrounding the birth of the policy, but because of the policies effectiveness they have said little since that time. The policy evolved secretly in the wake of the Chinese government's crackdown on the democracy movement in China in 1989. Rather than openly support the democratic movement, by sending two envoys—Brent Scowcroft and Lawrence Eagleburger—to assure the leaders of China, irrespective of the decisions to massacre their own citizens, President George H.W. decided to continue to engage the Chinese leadership.[138] Since that time the engagement policy continued to evolve under Clinton and thereafter during the administration of George W. Bush. While Obama is expected to place his own stamp on the policy of engagement, in the end the new president is unlikely to stray too far from the established norms that have undergirded the policy.

Step Two: If there is an area where President Obama can be innovative, an attempt to distinguish his policy from the past three presidents, he should use China to promote his environmental agenda. There are two issues that can advance Obama's green agenda: Global Warming and E-Waste. On the issue of Global Warming, in the post-Kyoto discussions, Obama can impress upon the Chinese that not only will the United States government join in any future global warming convention, but he will work to make it happen. Similarly, Obama will have to make it clear that China's active participation and its efforts to control its emission standards is critical to demonstrate to the world that they are serious in carrying out any measures in future environmental agreements. Taken collectively, these issues are a win-win for the President and China. In the final analysis President Obama will be positioned to meet a campaign objective on climate change: "That the United States, China, and other countries around the globe can and must cooperate to combat climate change and to create more secure, affordable, and dependable energy supplies. It also requires that China conduct its overseas exploration for oil in ways that do not interfere with international markets or undercut global standards for governance and investment."[139]

Will Obama and his "green team" raise the issue of E-Waste in China? The Basel Action Network and Silicon Valley Toxics Coalition have estimated that nearly 70 percent of the world's high-tech waste is exported or dumped in Asia. Similarly 90 percent of this waste flows into China. This is a perfect issue that helps both the Obama administration and the Hu government. First it allows both countries to work together on an issue that could forge closer ties. Second, China, with the assistance of the US government, could dramatically curtail, and one would hope, end the flow of e-waste, pollution and the resulting health effects to the Chinese citizens, and to those in other Asian countries. Viewed collectively, in the aforementioned areas, through engagement with China, Obama can use these issues to advance the president's green agenda.

Step Three: War, should it come, will develop over the issue of Taiwan. That is if Taiwan were to seek independence there is no doubt China would see such a move as an act of war. Taiwan is unlikely to seek independence at this time, primarily because President Ma Ying-jeou continues to embrace strong bilateral relations with mainland China. This point notwithstanding, given the inexperience of President Obama, one should anticipate a test from China on the issue of Taiwan. President Hu and the military in China will certainly want know to what extent, and under what circumstances, will Obama defend Taiwan. For example, China bristled over Bush's decision to provide advanced weapons to Taiwan. Despite protests from China President Bush remained firm. The point remains: under what circumstances and to what extent will President Obama defend Taiwan? If and when prompted by a crisis, or if Obama makes a statement proactively of support of Taiwan, anticipate a mini-crisis whereby China will test Obama's resolve.

Step Four: Retain China as ally in the war on terror. The Bush administration made extensive use of China in the war on terror. To be sure China is not now, nor will ever be a major partner in the current conflict, but the US government understands the role performed by Beijing. In particular China assisted the war effort in a number of ways: they pushed Pervez Musharraf to cooperate with the Bush administration in the wake of the tragic events of September 11, 2001; China has made efforts to provide economic assistance to Hamid Karsai's government in Afghanistan; and finally, the aforementioned bilateral efforts notwithstanding, the multilateral effort involving China in the six-party talks to prevent proliferation in the Korean peninsula has proven vital. This ongoing aspect of the Sino-American relationship should be retained and enhanced if the war on terror is to succeed in Asia. President Obama and his foreign policy team should utilize this mechanism to expand the relationship. Obama made a promising comment during the presidential campaign: "In Asia, the emergence of an economically vibrant, more politically active China offers new opportunities for prosperity and cooperation, but also poses new challenges for the United States and our partners in the region. It is time for the United States to take a more active role here–to build on our strong bilateral relations and informal arrangements like the Six Party talks. As President, I intend to forge a more effective regional framework in Asia that will promote stability, prosperity and help us confront common transnational threats such as tracking down terrorists and responding to global health problems like avian flu."[140]

What is clear is that taken collectively the aforementioned hinge threats are not going away. Management of them will be a critical barometer of President Obama's ability to deal with the major challenges to American leadership. Mistakes with India will not lead to war; this is true with regard to China, accept in the case of Taiwan. However, mistakes with Russia could lead to increased tensions and possibly conflict. Rest assured foreign policy watchers will observe these relationships as a critical measure of the success or failure of Obama's stewardship of US foreign policy.

CHAPTER 5
IRAQ: OBAMA'S POTENTIAL NIGHTMARE

Obama's statements on Iraq have undergone a dramatic transformation. That said one statement remained constant and symbolized the essence of his policy: "To renew American leadership in the world, we must first bring the Iraq war to a responsible end and refocus our attention"[141] to other issues in the region and around the world. Central to this shift in policy concerned the use of the savings on the costly Iraq adventure, and then use the funds for the president's domestic agenda. This chapter argues that there are a dangerous set of issues afoot: too quick a withdrawal may endanger gains already made on the ground and will almost certainly unleash a new round of sectarian violence and renew Al Qaeda's objective of establishing an operational base in Iraq. These dilemmas have additional consequences that will impact the Obama administration: having reduced US forces in Iraq will President Obama have the resolve to increase US troops if al Qaeda or Moghtada Al-Sadar's Madhi Army become resurgent? How will the increase in US forces impact the president's mandate to fix the economy? Finally, have these issues set the stage for a one-term presidency?

BUSH'S TRENDING PATH IN IRAQ: FROM QUAGMIRE TO POSSIBLE VICTORY

The Bush administrations preventive war produced domestic and international outrage. While Operation Iraqi Freedom successfully ended the oppressive regime of Saddam Hussein and allowed Iraqi's to pursue a democratic system, critics viewed the war as "unjust" and a "war of choice." The war produced a number of consequences. It increased antiwar activism world-wide. Second, the war ended US moral authority to conduct the war on terror. Third, the shift to Iraq allowed the Taliban and Al Qaeda to regroup in Afghanistan. Fourth, the Iraq War dominated the Bush presidency and destroyed his creditability with the American people. Lastly, the conduct of the postwar phase contributed to an expansive insurgency that many assert created a quagmire.

The use of the word quagmire emerged as a result of series of postwar dilemmas in Iraq. There were a number of indicators that invalidated the Bush administrations optimistic assessment that US forces would be in Iraq for a short period. By the fall of 2003 the administration refused to use the word "insurgency" even if there was evidence to validate the presence of burgeoning anti-Americanism across Iraq. Unwilling to admit that insurgents were responsible for the postwar chaos and the mounting civilian and American military deaths in Iraq, new descriptions of what the Bush administration was confronting began to surface. President Bush opined that Iraq "will be difficult" but in the end he asserted "we will win." Secretary of Defense Donald Rumsfeld commented that "we are in for a long hard slog." This statement served as a clear indicator that things were not going well in Iraq. These statements notwithstanding those that opposed the war had little fear in using the word quagmire. Many among the anti-war movement went one step further, asserting that the Iraq war is lost.

> In fact, it may already be too late to prevent Iraq from exploding. Iraq's new government is stuck in a fatal Catch-22: To have any credibility among Iraqis it must break with the US and oppose the occupation, but it couldn't last a week without the protection of American troops. The Bush administration is also stuck. Its failure to stabilize Iraq, and the continuing casualties there, have led to a steady slide in the president's popularity: Polls show that a majority of Americans no longer think that the war in Iraq was worth fighting in the first place. Yet withdrawing from Iraq would only lead to more chaos, and the rest of the world has exhibited little interest in cleaning up America's mess. Of the two dozen or so countries that sent troops to Iraq, fewer and fewer remain: Spain, Portugal, Hungary and New Zealand have already quit, and the Netherlands, Bulgaria, Ukraine and Italy have announced they are getting out. Even if the United Nations agreed to step in, there is little or no chance that the administration will internationalize control over Iraq. In the face of a full-scale civil war in Iraq, says a source close to the US military, Bush intends to go it alone.[142]

Undaunted by the criticism from the media, and the repeated polls that indicated the American people had grown tired of the war, President Bush pressed forward with his optimistic appraisal of events in postwar Iraq. On May 22, 2006 President Bush acknowledged "Years from now, people will look back on the formation of a unity government in Iraq as a decisive moment in the story of liberty, a moment when freedom gained a firm foothold in the Middle East and the forces of terror began their long retreat."[143] The president's statement proved problematic because internal reports within the administration indicated that Iraq continued to spiral downward. In one example, two days after Bush's speech, the intelligence division of the Joint Chiefs of Staff, according to Bob Woodward, circulated a secret intelligence appraisal that undercut Bush's statement. Rather than a decline of violence in Iraq, the report concluded that there would be an increase in violence in 2007. Thus according to the report "Insurgents and terrorists retain the resources and capabilities to sustain and even increase current levels of violence through the next year."[144]

Apparently the internal report was ignored because five months later President Bush continued his optimistic appraisal of the war. In a radio address on September 2, 2006 the president asserted "The security of the civilized world depends on victory in the war on terror, and that depends on victory in Iraq, so America will not leave until victory is achieved."[145] The reason the statement induced a negative reaction is that in the midst of an expanding insurgency, and with mounting US casualties, many Americans had grown increasingly tired of Bush's rhetoric. In a classic example in December of 2008 President Bush released "Our National Strategy for

Victory in Iraq." The document described a strategy that demonstrates that over a period of time Iraqi security forces were capable of taking the fight to the insurgents, and thereby paved the way for the prospect of US troops to commence exiting Iraq within a 12 month period. For the anti-war left, and for the majority of Americans, the public clamored for a strategy that called for withdrawal, or perhaps a clear strategy that would allow the United States to exit Iraq with honor.

In the 2006 congressional elections the Democratic Party used the anti-war movement as a critical voting block in its bid to control the US Congress. In control of both chambers the Democrats pressed forward with a central component of their agenda: ending the Iraq War. Those efforts failed for a number of reasons. The Democrats were unable to convince enough Republicans to vote in favor of cutting off funds for the war, and second the "surge strategy" reversed a trend that called for ending the war. While critics, including those in the Pentagon, concluded the surge would fail, the strategy succeeded beyond the imagination of its architects. The counterinsurgency plan called for the deployment of 30, 000 additional forces to Iraq. The bulk of these forces would be dispatched to the center of gravity of the war, Baghdad, which is not just the capital and political center of the country, but the sectarian "fault line" that crisscrossed the city.[146]

The success of the surge is measured in a number of ways. The sectarian violence in Iraq continued to decline. Second, Al Qaeda in Iraq (AQI) is all but defeated and its leadership structure is in disarray. Third, the surge benefited from internal factors: the Al Anbar Awakening and the fact that Sunni Iraqi's continued to actively join the political process are significant contributing factors. Similarly, the fact the Shiite Militias, led by Moqtada al-Sadr's Madhi Army, suspended operations (and when they challenged US and coalition forces they were quickly defeated) is another factor that assisted in lowering the threat to US forces. Finally, another measure of the success is that with violence declining (non-extent in many parts of Iraq), US forces have returned authority of many provinces formerly under American control to Iraqi forces. To provide a vivid example, of the changing tide in Iraq, in January of 2009, in perhaps the most significant validation of success of the surge, the US military handed over authority of the "Green Zone" to the Iraq Forces.

OBAMA AND IRAQ

Barack Obama's perspective on the war in Iraq did not begin, as many think, after the war commenced. Rather, then Illinois State Senator Barack Obama, at what was Chicago's first high-profile anti-Iraq war rally at the Federal Plaza in Chicago, Illinois, on October 2, 2002 (an event that coincided with the announcement by President Bush and Congress on an agreement on the joint resolution authorizing the Iraq War), made his position clear before the commencement of the war. The following excerpt provides a glimpse into the thinking, indeed the passions expressed during State Senator Obama's anti-war address:

> I don't oppose all wars. And I know that in this crowd today, there is no shortage of patriots, or of patriotism. What I am opposed to is a dumb war. What I am opposed to is a rash war. What I am opposed to is the cynical attempt by Richard Perle and Paul Wolfowitz and other arm-chair, weekend warriors in this Administration to shove their

own ideological agendas down our throats, irrespective of the costs in lives lost and in hardships borne. What I am opposed to is the attempt by political hacks like Karl Rove to distract us from a rise in the uninsured, a rise in the poverty rate, a drop in the median income—to distract us from corporate scandals and a stock market that has just gone through the worst month since the Great Depression. That's what I'm opposed to. A dumb war. A rash war. A war based not on reason but on passion, not on principle but on politics. Now let me be clear—I suffer no illusions about Saddam Hussein. He is a brutal man. A ruthless man. A man who butchers his own people to secure his own power. He has repeatedly defied UN resolutions, thwarted UN inspection teams, developed chemical and biological weapons, and coveted nuclear capacity. He's a bad guy. The world, and the Iraqi people, would be better off without him. But I also know that Saddam poses no imminent and direct threat to the United States, or to his neighbors, that the Iraqi economy is in shambles, that the Iraqi military a fraction of its former strength, and that in concert with the international community he can be contained until, in the way of all petty dictators, he falls away into the dustbin of history. I know that even a successful war against Iraq will require a US occupation of undetermined length, at undetermined cost, with undetermined consequences. I know that an invasion of Iraq without a clear rationale and without strong international support will only fan the flames of the Middle East, and encourage the worst, rather than best, impulses of the Arab world, and strengthen the recruitment arm of Al Qaeda.[147]

The anti-war speech was a local event and therefore received no national coverage. During Obama's US Senate bid the state senator repeatedly referred to his "early" opposition to Iraq war. Indeed his position on the war became the centerpiece of his senate campaign strategy. Having become the junior senator representing the state of Illinois in Washington, DC, whenever the opportunity developed Barack Obama would use his position as a member of the senate foreign relations committee as a pulpit to vocalize his anti-Iraq War stance. Similarly, he understandably used this forum as a means to criticize the Bush administrations policy in Iraq.

The senate foreign relations committee was by no means the only forum that Barack Obama used to express his anti-Iraq War views. In remarks made to the Chicago Council on Global Affairs on November 20, 2006, in an address titled "A Way Forward in Iraq," Obama used the occasion to once again criticize President Bush's policies in Iraq.

These are serious times for our country, and … Americans demanded a feasible strategy with defined goals in Iraq–a strategy no longer driven by ideology and politics, but one that is based on a realistic assessment of the sobering facts on the ground and our interests in the region. This kind of realism has been missing since the very conception of this war, and it is what led me to publicly oppose it in 2002. The notion that Iraq would quickly and easily become a bulwark of flourishing democracy in the Middle East was not a plan for victory, but an ideological fantasy. I said then and believe now that Saddam Hussein was a ruthless dictator who craved weapons of mass destruction but posed no imminent threat to the United States; that a war in Iraq would harm, not help, our efforts to defeat al Qaeda and finish the job in Afghanistan; and that an invasion would require an occupation of undetermined length, at undetermined cost, with undetermined consequences. Month after month, and then year after year, I've watched with a heavy heart as my deepest suspicions about this war's conception have been confirmed and exacerbated in its disastrous implementation. No matter how bad it gets, we are told to wait, and not ask questions. We have been assured that the insurgency is in its last throes. We have been told that progress is just around the corner, and that when the Iraqis stand up, we will be able to stand down. Last week, without a trace of irony, the President even chose Vietnam as the backdrop for remarks counseling "patience" with his policies in Iraq. When I came here and gave a speech on this war a year ago, I suggested that we begin to move towards a phased redeployment of American troops from Iraqi soil. At that point, seventy-five US Senators, Republican and Democrat, including myself, had also voted in favor of a resolution demanding that 2006 be a year of significant transition in Iraq. What we have seen instead is a year of significant deterioration. A year in which well-respected Republicans like John Warner, former Administration officials like Colin Powell, generals who have served in Iraq, and intelligence experts have all said that what we are doing is not working. A year that is ending with an attempt by the bipartisan Iraq Study Group to determine what can be done about a country that is quickly spiraling out of control.[148]

This address is revealing for a number of reasons. First, the address unveils a far more substantive critique of his opposition to the war. Second, the address details efforts by Obama to provide a clear movement, from his point of view, whereby he attempted to identify a bipartisan opposition to the Iraq War. With the Democrats in control of the Congress, Obama and other members of the Democratic Party became far more strident in their opposition to the war. In time the Democrats publically discussed their intentions to cut off funds (measures that failed) for the Iraq War.

In Barack Obama's speech announcing his 2008 run for the White House in Springfield, Illinois on February 10, 2007, for the first time the senator provided a specific date for ending the Iraq War: "It's time to start bringing our troops home. It's time to admit that no amount of American lives can resolve the political disagreement that lies at the heart of someone else's civil war. That's why I have a plan that will bring our combat troops home by March of 2008. Letting the Iraqis know that we will not be there forever is our last, best hope to pressure the Sunni and Shia to come to the table and find peace."[149] This speech marked the initial time Senator Barack Obama formerly declared a date for the complete withdrawal of American troops from Iraq. Quietly, Democrats viewed his declared date as "unrealistic," "naïve" and "unworkable." Thus while many among the Democratic Party establishment shared Obama's desire to remove US troops from Iraq, there was a sense that 2009 or later would prove far more workable.

In an interview with Tim Russert on November 2007 on the *NBC* program "Meet The Press," Obama clarified his position, acknowledging "I've been absolutely clear in terms of the approach that I would take. I would end this war, and I would have our troops out within 16 months."[150] Undaunted by the criticism of a clear shift, and in front of the senator's Chicago constituency, Obama pressed forward with his "old position" declaring to end US involvement in Iraq by March 2008. In an address titled "The American Moment," remarks made before The Chicago Council on Global Affairs on April 23, 2007, Obama observed

The first way America will lead is by bringing a responsible end to this war in Iraq and refocusing on the critical challenges in the broader region. In a speech five months ago,

I argued that there can be no military solution to what has become a political conflict between Sunni and Shi'a factions. And I laid out a plan that I still believe offers the best chance of pressuring these warring factions toward a political settlement—a phased withdrawal of American forces with the goal of removing all combat brigades from Iraq by March 31st, 2008. I acknowledged at the time that there are risks involved in such an approach. But my plan also makes clear that continued US commitment to Iraq depends on the Iraqi government meeting a series of well-defined benchmarks necessary to reach a political settlement. Thus far, the Iraqi government has made very little progress in meeting any of the benchmarks, in part because the President has refused time and again to tell the Iraqi government that we will not be there forever. The President's escalation of US forces may bring a temporary reduction in the violence in Baghdad, at the price of increased US casualties—though the experience so far is not encouraging. But it cannot change the political dynamic in Iraq. A phased withdrawal can. Moreover, until we change our approach in Iraq, it will be increasingly difficult to refocus our efforts on the challenges in the wider region—on the conflict in the Middle East, where Hamas and Hezbollah feel emboldened and Israel's prospects for a secure peace seem uncertain; on Iran, which has been strengthened by the war in Iraq; and on Afghanistan, where more American forces are needed to battle al Qaeda, track down Osama bin Laden, and stop that country from backsliding toward instability.[151]

The speech illustrated a shift away from the 16 month timetable. However, during the Democratic Primary debates Obama began to wither in the face of criticism and questions about his selected date for ending the Iraq War. In the Democratic Primary Debate Obama made a dramatic shift in his position on the US withdrawal from Iraq. The following exchange between *NBC*'s Tim Russert and Obama illustrate the intense pressure that developed over the senator's positions on Iraq.

Obama: If there are still large troop presences in—when I take office, then the first thing I will do is call together the Joint Chiefs of Staff and initiate a phased redeployment. We've got to be as careful getting out as we were careless getting in, but military personnel indicate we can get one brigade to two brigades out per month. I would immediately begin that process. We would get combat troops out of Iraq. The only troops that would remain would be those that have to protect US bases and US civilians, as well as to engage in counterterrorism activities in Iraq. The important principle, though, is there are not going to be any military solutions to the problem in Iraq. There has to be a political accommodation, and the best way for us to support the troops and to stabilize the situation in Iraq is to begin that phased redeployment.

Russert: Will you pledge that by January 2013, the end of your first term, more than five years from now, there will be no US troops in Iraq?

Obama: I think it's hard to project four years from now, and I think it would be irresponsible. We don't know what contingency will be out there. What I can promise is that if there are still troops in Iraq when I take office—which it appears there may be, unless we can get some of our Republican colleagues to change their mind and cut off funding without a timetable—if there's no timetable—then I will drastically reduce our presence there to the mission of protecting our embassy, protecting our civilians, and making sure that we're carrying out counterterrorism activities there. I believe that we should have all our troops out by 2013, but I don't want to make promises, not knowing what the situation's going to be three or four years out.[152]

In accepting the political reality that the March 2008 withdrawal date of American troops had impacted his campaign for the presidency, in yet another foreign policy speech Obama made a determined effort not to discuss the topic (withdrawal date) at all. Instead, he used the address to sharpen his criticism of the costs incurred by the Iraq War, and why, as a result of President Bush's mismanagement of the war, he should be next commander-in-chief. In an address aptly titled "The World Beyond Iraq," on March 19, 2008, Obama observed, "Five years have gone by since that fateful decision. This war has now lasted longer than World War I, World War II, or the Civil War. Nearly four thousand Americans have given their lives. Thousands more have been wounded. Even under the best case scenarios, this war will cost American taxpayers well over a trillion dollars. And where are we for all of this sacrifice? We are less safe and less able to shape events abroad. We are divided at home, and our alliances around the world have been strained. The threats of a new century have roiled the waters of peace and stability, and yet America remains anchored in Iraq. History will catalog the reasons why we waged a war that didn't need to be fought, but two stand out. In 2002, when the fateful decisions about Iraq were made, there was a President for whom ideology overrode pragmatism, and there were too many politicians in Washington who spent too little time reading the intelligence reports, and too much time reading public opinion."[153] Thereafter, Obama made the case for why he should be the next president: "The lesson of Iraq is that when we are making decisions about matters as grave as war, we need a policy rooted in reason and facts, not ideology and politics. Now we are debating who should be our next Commander-in-Chief. And I am running for President because it's time to turn the page on a failed ideology and a fundamentally flawed political strategy, so that we can make pragmatic judgments to keep our country safe. That's what I did when I stood up and opposed this war from the start, and said that we needed to finish the fight against al Qaeda. And that's what I'll do as President of the United States."[154]

Obama's address had an added dimension: he indicated, from his perspective, why, in the candidates view, the Iraq war decreased rather than increased US security. According to Obama, "The war in Iraq has emboldened Iran, which poses the greatest challenge to American interests in the Middle East in a generation, continuing its nuclear program and threatening our ally, Israel. Instead of the new Middle East we were promised, Hamas runs Gaza, Hezbollah flags fly from the rooftops in Sadr City, and Iran is handing out money left and right in southern Lebanon. The war in Iraq has emboldened North Korea, which built new nuclear weapons and even tested one before the Administration finally went against its own rhetoric, and pursued diplomacy. The war in Iraq has emboldened the Taliban, which has rebuilt its strength since we took our eye off of Afghanistan. Above all, the war in Iraq has emboldened al Qaeda, whose recruitment has jumped and whose leadership enjoys a safe-haven in Pakistan—a thousand miles from Iraq."[155]

Important though the speech may have been Democrats and Republicans continued to pound Obama on the apparent shift in position. In the midst of the criticism Obama proffered another position. In an attempt to again clarify his position Obama appeared on *NBC*'s "Today" in April 8, 2008. In an interview with Meredith Vieira Obama was forced to address this issue head on. In a long set up of her question, Vieira observed, "You've said when, Senator. You've said if you are elected, that within 16 months you're going to bring all … troops home from Iraq. Senator McCain said yesterday that is a reckless promise that you cannot possibly keep; a failure of leadership. And even military leaders say that any withdrawal of troops would be dictated by security on the ground. So how can you guarantee you can pull out those troops in just 16 months?" In response Obama asserted, "Meredith, I've been very consistent in saying that we are going to set a timetable and we will have a prudent pace of withdrawal, one to two brigades per month. At that pace we can have combat troops out within approximately 16 months."[156]

The interview exposed two issues. First, politically there was an increasing recognition that Obama's position on the withdrawal of U.S troops from Iraq induced an impression that the senator was not ready to become commander-in-chief. Second, as an attendant consequence Obama found there was no escaping the subject. If and when Obama shifted to other issues, reporters or criticism from his political rivals kept the issue of his withdrawal of US troops in Iraq in the news. This proved difficult because Obama wanted domestic issues not foreign policy to be the focus of his campaign.

With the general election underway President Bush in September of 2008 announced the administration would reduce US troops in Iraq by 8,000 and he would dispatch 4,500 additional troops to Afghanistan. As one would expect both presidential candidates expressed their positions. Barack Obama's response linked Bush and Senator McCain not just to the failed policy in Iraq, but how the president's decisions in Iraq had consequences elsewhere. According to Obama, "What President Bush and Senator McCain don't understand is that the central front in the war on terror is not in Iraq, and it never was—the central front is in Afghanistan and Pakistan, where the terrorists who hit us on 9/11 are still plotting attacks seven years later. Today, the Taliban is on the offensive, al Qaeda has a new sanctuary, and its leaders are putting out videotapes. Yet under President Bush's plan, we still have nearly four times the number of troops in Iraq than Afghanistan, and we have no comprehensive plan to deal with the al Qaeda sanctuary in northwest Pakistan."[157]

McCain by contrast said little of substance about President Bush's announcement. Instead McCain blasted his political rival. According to McCain, "Senator Obama is utterly confused by the progress in the war in Iraq. He has minimized the success of the surge in stabilizing Iraq, but today said the reductions in violence exceeded expectations. The surge has greatly brought down violence, but Senator Obama would still oppose it, even in retrospect…. Today's announcement stands in clear contrast to the reckless approach long advocated by Senator Obama. His proposal—to withdraw forces based on a political timetable, no matter the consequences for Iraq or American national security—is profoundly irresponsible. Senator Obama's comments today demonstrate again his commitment to retreating from Iraq no matter what the cost. His focus is on withdrawal—not on victory…. It is clear that we need additional forces in Afghanistan, and I support the new deployments. Senator Obama believes we must lose in Iraq to win in Afghanistan. I want to win in Iraq and in Afghanistan. As we succeed in Iraq, we must also succeed in Afghanistan. I continue to have full confidence in Generals [David] Petraeus and [Ray] Odierno as they prepare to assume their new responsibilities, and I look forward to continuing to rely on their advice and counsel as we seek to prevail in both Iraq and Afghanistan."[158]

The deepening recession eclipsed any meaningful discussion about Iraq or other foreign policy issues. The last significant comment made by Obama on the subject of Iraq occurred during the presidential debate on October 7, 2008. For Obama the controversy surrounding the senators plans to withdraw US troops never surfaced in the debate. Rather, any discussion about Iraq, given the debate about the financial bailout in Washington, D.C., seemed out of place. Similarly, the success of the surge (even if the senator never thought it would work) made it easier for Obama to focus on the "costs" of the Iraq War. According to Obama, "So one of the difficulties with Iraq is that it has put an enormous strain, first of all, on our troops, obviously, and they have performed heroically and honorably and we owe them an extraordinary debt of gratitude. But it's also put an enormous strain on our budget. We've spent, so far, close to $700 billion and if we continue on the path that we're on, as Senator McCain is suggesting, it's going to go well over $1 trillion. We're spending $10 billion a month in Iraq at a time when the Iraqis have a $79 billion surplus, $79 billion. And we need that $10 billion a month here in the United States to put people back to work, to do all these wonderful things that Senator McCain suggested we should be doing, but has not yet explained how he would pay for."[159]

OBAMA AND DILEMMAS POSED BY IRAQ

From this point forward the objective is to demonstrate the potential nightmare posed by Iraq to President Obama. Long before the presidential election concluded a dilemma emerged for the Democratic Party. Prior to the surge Iraq offered the Democrats an issue that could be used against the eventual Republican presidential nominee in the general election. But because of the success of the surge the Democrat Party was hard pressed to cut funds for the war and second they did want to openly admit that the strategy worked, which meant they, including Obama, were wrong. This all proved even more unsettling for the Democrats when you consider Senate Majority Leader Harry Reid denounced the war in Iraq "as a lost cause." For Democratic strategists, the issue of Iraq offered so many tangible benefits, including linking Bush's failed war to John McCain, now it represented a host of problems.

With the success of the surge, Republicans were emboldened by the prospects for victory in Iraq. They too confronted a dilemma: How to use the good fortunes in Iraq to sustain the Republican hold over the White House? Given that the economy was in the tank, how could Senator McCain use Iraq to eclipse the increasingly moribund economy? It was this dilemma that was a contributing factor that cost McCain the presidency. In the summer of 2008 many conservatives thought it important to ignore the dilemma posed by Iraq to the Republican Party, and instead focus on the problems the surge presented to the Democratic Party. William Rusher, for example, opined "It seems likely that George W. Bush will achieve his goal of stepping down as president with the Iraq problem well on its way to a solution. That leaves the Democrats in a bit of a pickle. What, exactly, is their current policy on Iraq? It would be out of the question to insist, in the teeth of the good news from Iraq, that the United States should adopt the former Democratic policy and simply bug out. And, in purely political terms, it would be equally difficult for the Democrats to admit they were wrong, reverse their position and endorse the administration policy."[160]

How did it come to this? That is how did the Democrat's end up in such a precarious position? In truth Iraq always posed a dilemma for the Democratic Party? For starters when it appeared that President Bush's war aims were based on obfuscation, a fact that was validated when the administration could not locate Saddam Hussein's alleged weapons of mass destruction, the Democrats were in no position to end the war. Second, as the insurgency took hold in Iraq and the casualties increased among US forces, the Democrats were limited to criticizing President Bush for not having a coherent postwar strategy. As the 2006 congressional elections approached, the Democrats were on the verge of regaining control of the Congress, but Iraq would again pose a dilemma. Eric Alterman expressed the dilemma this way:

> Many on the left are demanding that the Democrats adopt an "out now" policy toward Iraq, but this, too, misunderstands the party's political problem. First off, it's not practical. Even if the leadership were to sign on to an out-now strategy, it has no enforcement mechanism to insure the compliance of those who disagree. The effect would undoubtedly be to reinforce the "disarray/these people can't be trusted to protect us" narrative that remains the Democrats' Achilles' heel. What's more, despite growing public support, a call for withdrawal would be treated in the conservative punditocracy as the equivalent of a call to "cut and run," and hence would open the entire "weak on defense" Pandora's Box that almost always dooms Democrats in national elections. And for what? Does anyone truly believe that if the Democratic leadership calls for Bush to quit Iraq, it will actually happen? Nevertheless, it's an awful situation, and all attempts to address it will be fraught with risk. A Democratic refusal to adopt a single position on Iraq collides, strategically, not only with growing dissatisfaction and impatience with the failed Bush strategy there but also with the need for Democrats to nationalize the 2006 election in order to focus attention on Republican incompetence, corruption and ideological extremism.[161]

If the Democrats had a dilemma in Iraq, it therefore follows that Senator Obama had a problem as well: "The widespread conviction among Democrats that we are destined to fail in Iraq was the key to Barack Obama's emergence as Presidential front-runner. He postured himself as the candidate who had opposed the war from the beginning. But what helped Obama in the Democratic primaries may prove his undoing...."[162] The dilemma of Iraq manifested itself in other ways for Obama. As a state senator Obama joined the antiwar protesters and he adroitly articulated why President Bush's decision to launch a war that unseated the oppressive regime of Saddam Hussein undermined the real war against al Qaeda, but during the presidential campaign Obama's Iraq dilemma became more acute. The dilemma, as describe in greater detail above, in this context is that Obama could not provide a precise timetable for when he would withdraw US troops from Iraq. In announcing his presidential bid on February 10, 2007 Obama observed "I have a plan that will bring our combat troops home by March of 2008." After this date was met with criticism, Obama's date for ending the war underwent a transformation. Rather than March of 2008, Obama instead spoke of "having combat troops out within approximately 16 months" after he entered the White House. That position faced opposition. In the Presidential Primary Debate on September 26, 2007 the dilemma of Iraq resurfaced. In the interview Tim Russert pressed Obama to commit to having US troops out by 2013. Rather than accepting a formal commitment date Obama wavered stating that "I believe that we should have all our troops out by 2013, but I don't want to make promises, not knowing what the situation's going to be three or four years out."[163] His response, had he not had other positions, would have been appropriate under normal circumstances. However, with Iraq showing dramatic improvement any change was viewed in many quarters as "political" or "a flip-flop." Finally, the multiple positions on ending the Iraq War exposed two issues: either he was pandering to the left wing of the Democratic Party for votes, or when pressed by critics that his date of withdrawal threatened the gains in Iraq to end the criticism Obama wavered providing a far less precise "end date."

Obama's Iraq dilemma manifested itself in other ways. The dilemma exposed a not so quiet rift within Obama's expansive coalition; second, Iraq unveiled Obama's Nixonian dilemma, and finally, the closing portion of the chapter will illustrate why Iraq could develop into a potential nightmare for President Obama.

Long before Obama entered the White House there were clear signs the natives (a reference to the left-wing of the Democratic Party) were becoming restless. Much of the pessimism had to do with Obama's foreign policy selections: "Mr. Obama has moved quickly in the last 48 hours to get his cabinet team in place, unveiling a raft of heavyweight appointments, in addition to Hillary Clinton as his Secretary of State. But his preference for General James Jones, a former NATO commander who backed John McCain, as his National Security Adviser and Arizona Governor Janet Napolitano, a supporter of the war, to run the Homeland Security department has dismayed many of his earliest supporters. The likelihood that Mr. Obama will retain George W. Bush's Defense Secretary, Robert Gates, has reinforced the notion that he will not aggressively pursue the radical withdrawal of all combat troops from Iraq over the next 16 months and engagement with rogue states that he has pledged."[164] This decision set off alarmed bells in a critical component of the President Obama's coalition. In response to Obama's foreign policy selections, Chris Bowers of the high profile OpenLeft.com blog, expressed disappointment: "That is, over all, a centre-right foreign policy team. I feel incredibly frustrated. Progressives are being entirely left out of Obama's major appointments so far."[165]

Obama's inclusion of hawks, and former members of the Bush administration, according to David J. Rothkopf, is representative of the "violin model," which translates this way: "Hold power with the left hand, and play the music with your right. It's teaching us something about Obama: while he wants to bring new ideas to the game, he is working from the center space of American foreign policy."[166]

Perhaps one of Obama's most depressing dilemmas as a result of his end game strategy in Iraq is the parallels to Nixon. At issue, what are those comparisons and how do they validate Obama's problems in Iraq? There is another central question: Will the Ghost of Richard Nixon Haunt the Obama White House?

These queries are not all that far fetched, nor do they represent political or intellectual discourse of the moment. In its most rudimentary terms, the comparison is sadly based on all too familiar facts. For starters in 1968 the moment Nixon entered office the Vietnam War became his war. Having entered the White House as the 44th President of the United States on January 20, 2009 the Iraq War, formerly Bush's War is now Obama's War. There are, however, far more significant parallels. According to Brian R. Robertson, "Nixon largely avoided establishing a clear position on Vietnam while promising to pursue a "peace with honor," and Obama promises to "responsibly end the war in Iraq." Both, moreover, sought the advice of Henry Kissinger. Jeffrey Kimball, the eminent scholar on Nixon and the Vietnam War, revealed that Nixon hoped his credentials as a career anti-communist and potential nuclear threats against North Vietnam and the Soviet Union would force the North Vietnamese to agree to a cease-fire. Nixon based this approach on the belief that Eisenhower's nuclear threats toward China and North Korea forced both countries to sue for a cease-fire (though recent scholarship suggests that Stalin's death played a principal factor in North Korea's, China's and, the Soviet Union's decision to agree to a cease-fire). Obama, on the other hand, campaigned on a promise to "press Iraq's leaders to take responsibility for their future and to substantially spend their oil revenues on their own reconstruction," and "increase stability in Iraq by launching "an aggressive diplomatic effort to reach a comprehensive compact on the stability of Iraq and the region."[167]

The comparisons do not end there. For certain President Obama will confront similar challenges that impacted Nixon in 1968. Here are perhaps the most significant parallels:

> Popular support for the war in Iraq has reached an all-time low. And he faces the decision of whether to cut our losses or to basically continue the policy of the Bush administration. With many policy experts concluding that the US troop surge has been successful, Obama will have little incentive to choose an alternative approach to Iraq. To further complicate matters, if Obama does choose to withdraw US troops too quickly from Iraq, there is a good chance that the Iraqi government will collapse and the region will become further destabilized. There can be little doubt that if Iraq did fall Obama would have to struggle to convince Americans to support his policies. The political fallout could damage his chances for reelection in 2012.… Some may argue that Obama has the advantage of working with a Congress and Senate controlled by the Democrats (whereas Nixon faced a Congress controlled by the opposing political party). The Democratic controlled Congress, however, has done very little to restrict President George W. Bush's prosecution of the war. In fact, last summer, the Democratic controlled Congress appropriated $162 billion dollars to continue the wars in Iraq and Afghanistan. Just as "Johnson's war" became "Nixon's War," "Bush's War" could very easily become "Obama's War.… Because the price of a loss in Iraq would be high, Obama will feel pressure to continue Bush's Iraq policy of "Iraqifying" the war.…[168]

These issues are certain to be scrutinized as President Obama's policy in Iraq unfolds. One will stand out: Nixon succeeded in his Vietnamization of the Vietnam War but he not only expanded the conflict into Cambodia and Laos, in the end he lost a war he inherited from his predecessor President Johnson. For all of Nixon's rhetoric about Johnson's failed conduct of war matters were made worse during his tenure. For Obama he too lambasted his predecessor, President Bush, for his abysmal conduct of the postwar reconstruction period in Iraq. Through the surge Bush succeeded in an area—Iraqification—where he had previously failed. In Obama's attempt to implement his campaign pledge to withdraw US forces, the world will closely watch the unfolding realities of the new president's Iraqification policy.

Obama's Iraqification policy was revealed on February 27, 2009 in a speech to US Marines at Camp Lejeune, North Carolina. During the speech President Obama stated that "I have come to speak to you about how the war in Iraq will end." Other significant aspects of the speech include the following:

> To understand where we need to go in Iraq, it is important for the American people to understand where we now stand. Thanks in great measure to your service, the situation in Iraq has improved. Violence has been reduced substantially from the horrific sectarian killing of 2006 and 2007. Al Qaeda in Iraq has been dealt a serious blow by our troops and Iraq's Security Forces, and through our partnership with Sunni Arabs.

The capacity of Iraq's Security Forces has improved, and Iraq's leaders have taken steps toward political accommodation. The relative peace and strong participation in January's provincial elections sent a powerful message to the world about how far Iraqis have come in pursuing their aspirations through a peaceful political process. On my first full day in office, I directed my national security team to undertake a comprehensive review of our strategy in Iraq to determine the best way to strengthen that foundation, while strengthening American national security. I have listened to my Secretary of Defense, the Joint Chiefs of Staff, and commanders on the ground. We have acted with careful consideration of events on the ground; with respect for the security agreements between the United States and Iraq; and with a critical recognition that the long-term solution in Iraq must be political—not military. Because the most important decisions that have to be made about Iraq's future must now be made by Iraqis. We have also taken into account the simple reality that America can no longer afford to see Iraq in isolation from other priorities: we face the challenge of refocusing on Afghanistan and Pakistan; of relieving the burden on our military; and of rebuilding our struggling economy—and these are challenges that we will meet. Today, I can announce that our review is complete, and that the United States will pursue a new strategy to end the war in Iraq through a transition to full Iraqi responsibility. This strategy is grounded in a clear and achievable goal shared by the Iraqi people and the American people: an Iraq that is sovereign, stable, and self-reliant. To achieve that goal, we will work to promote an Iraqi government that is just, representative, and accountable, and that provides neither support nor safe-haven to terrorists. We will help Iraq build new ties of trade and commerce with the world. And we will forge a partnership with the people and government of Iraq that contributes to the peace and security of the region. What we will not do is let the pursuit of the perfect stand in the way of achievable goals. We cannot rid Iraq of all who oppose America or sympathize with our adversaries. We cannot police Iraq's streets until they are completely safe, nor stay until Iraq's union is perfected. We cannot sustain indefinitely a commitment that has put a strain on our military, and will cost the American people nearly a trillion dollars. America's men and women in uniform have fought block by block, province by province, year after year, to give the Iraqis this chance to choose a better future. Now, we must ask the Iraqi people to seize it. The first part of this strategy is therefore the responsible removal of our combat brigades from Iraq. As a candidate for President, I made clear my support for a timeline of 16 months to carry out this drawdown, while pledging to consult closely with our military commanders upon taking office to ensure that we preserve the gains we've made and protect our troops. Those consultations are now complete, and I have chosen a timeline that will remove our combat brigades over the next 18 months. Let me say this as plainly as I can: by August 31, 2010, our combat mission in Iraq will end. As we carry out this drawdown, my highest priority will be the safety and security of our troops and civilians in Iraq. We will proceed carefully, and I will consult closely with my military commanders on the ground and with the Iraqi government. There will surely be difficult periods and tactical adjustments. But our enemies should be left with no doubt: this plan gives our military the forces and the flexibility they need to support our Iraqi partners, and to succeed. I intend to remove all US troops from Iraq by the end of 2011. We will complete this transition to Iraqi responsibility, and we will bring our troops home with the honor that they have earned.[169]

The address was mixed. Critics on the left, including House Speaker Nancy Pelosi, and other members of the Democratic Party, and anti-war activists, were outraged by this portion of the president's speech: "After we remove our combat brigades, our mission will change from combat to supporting the Iraqi government and its Security Forces as they take the absolute lead in securing their country. As I have long said, we will retain a transitional force to carry out three distinct functions: training, equipping, and advising Iraqi Security Forces as long as they remain non-sectarian; conducting targeted counter-terrorism missions; and protecting our ongoing civilian and military efforts within Iraq. Initially, this force will likely be made up of 35-50, 000 US troops."[170] The reality among the left wing of Democratic Party is that President Obama abandoned his pledge to remove "all US troops."

Proponents of the speech were thrilled with the flexibility demonstrated by President Obama. That is Obama appears to have listened to military commanders concerns about leaving a residual force to deal with contingencies. Senator John McCain thought the decision to remove US troops in 2011 was "responsible." Former aides to President Bush were equally delighted by the speech. In one example Gordon D. Johndroe, Bush's last national security spokesman, made this statement: "The specific timing is only slightly different but consistent with the goal of helping Iraq become self-sufficient in providing its own security. This is possible because of the success of the surge."[171] At issue is 35, 000-50,000 significant enough to deal with future violence in Iraq?

The decision to set a timetable for ending the US mission in Iraq increased rather decreased Obama's Iraq dilemma. Indeed the president's Iraq dilemma may evolve into other more damaging dimensions. Within the Middle East there will be strong pressures, particularly from Saudi Arabia and Egypt that will insist on a large US troop presence in Iraq to prevent a future advance or expansion of Iran's Shiite revolution. This translates into the need to keep US troops in Iraq past the 2011 deadline. At another level there will be strong pressures from within the military and from the Congress that will privately seek a "snails place" withdrawal to protect Iraq's fledgling democracy from the remaining elements of Al Qaeda in Iraq or the Madhi Army which has been laying low awaiting Obama's announced American troop exit plans in the hopes of not only filling a vacuum, but ultimately completing their long held objective of installing a radical Islamic Government, thereby ending secularism in Iraq. Though it is unlikely that forces loyal to Osama bin Laden or Moghtada Al-Sadar are likely to succeed in unseating the current or a future government in Iraq, both forces, should President Obama drastically reduce US forces, there is little doubt that insurgent violence will increase, threatening the military and political gains occurred under the "surge." Should this scenario come to pass, will President Obama, who campaigned to end the Iraq War, now have the political skill to re-engage US troops? Having made this decision, there will be those that will suggest that Obama's assorted Iraq dilemmas may threaten not only his reelection but may induce a reoccurring nightmare. In a concluding caveat author Thomas Ricks wrote these memorable words in his book *The Gamble: General David Petraeus and the American Military Adventure in Iraq, 2006-2008* that should be considered by President Obama: "The events for which the Iraq war will be remembered probably have not yet happened."[172]

CHAPTER 6
OBAMA AND THE MIDDLE EAST

President Obama has maintained that Iraq is a distraction from a far more significant set of concerns. On this point the president said the following: [I will] "bring the Iraq war to a responsible end and refocus our attention on the broader Middle East."[173] High on the president's regional agenda concerns the need to resolve the Palestinian-Israeli dispute. On this point Obama made the following statement: "This moment is an opportunity to let Palestinians know that we will work toward the goal of achieving a viable, democratic Palestinian state in the West Bank and Gaza living side by side with Israel and peace and security, but that this goal can only be achieved through acceptance of Israel and a commitment to non-violence."[174] This chapter demonstrates that Obama's Middle East strategy in many ways will be a continuation of the approach of former President Bill Clinton. Similarly, much like his Democratic predecessor, Obama intends to use political capital to obtain an agreement. This chapter assesses the prospects for and impediments to peace during the Obama presidency.

THE REALITIES OF MIDDLE EASTERN POLITICS

Consistent with the post-September 11 realities President Bush concluded the time had arrived to try again to push for an expansive Middle East peace Initiative. This time the US effort, according to Bush, would be far more comprehensive and the participants, the people and leaders within the region, would be far more engaged in the process.

The Middle East policy initiatives of the Bush presidency were informed by a number of assumptions. The first assumption asserted the status quo proved unacceptable. The "old way" of doing things recognized the dilemmas posed by coddling repressive regimes was deemed acceptable. Under Bush the president and his senior aides concluded the support for authoritarian regimes would no longer find acceptance in the region; the president asserted that repressive policies and human rights abuses were morally reprehensible and that anti-democratic practices and the support of them did little to increase stability in the region.

With regard to the second assumption, senior officials—the neoconservatives in particular—inside the Bush administration strongly acknowledged that Iraq's weapons of mass destruction posed an unacceptable risk to US regional interests. Third, because of Clinton's failures to enact a grand peace settlement in the region, Bush pursued a hands-off approach preferring to wait for a signal from the major parties before risking his and US reputation in the pursuit of an agreement. In the fourth and final assumption, to reduce the ever-present problems posed by terrorism, and ensure a long term regional stability, Bush and his senior aides concluded that democratization was critical to stability in the region.[175]

The four assumptions outlined above set the stage for President Bush's efforts to reshape the Middle East. The president enlisted another variable to buttress the administrations efforts to reshape the region: the use of force.

In an examination of the Bush administrations efforts to reshape the tempestuous region what is clear is that the four assumptions represented a break from the past, but in the end the new strategy was marked by set backs. Oddly the war on terror undercut the president's desire to rid the region of repressive regimes. In short, the war on terror, the need for partners with specific skills, particularly in the area of torture, that collectively overshadowed any hope of riding the region of repressive regimes. Second, weapons of mass destruction are indeed a threat to US interests in the region, but because the administration did not locate any in Iraq, a key war aim for the Iraq War dissipated, and critics assert the American image and moral authority to conduct the war on terror suffered a major hit. Third, with regard to peace efforts, The Road Map to Peace fizzled and the Annapolis conference amounted to a grand photo opportunity and little else. Finally, in the area of exporting democracy in the region, this too had mixed results. There is little doubt democracy is taking hold in Iraq; the evidence is in part due to a series of historic elections, and the development of political parties and civil institutions. In Lebanon democratic elections have taken place, but Hezbollah's influence in the south and Syria's efforts to retain Lebanon as a colony indicates that country is a weak state. In the final analysis, the realities of the region demonstrate that despite evidence of democratization the Middle East is still influenced by Islamic fundamentalism and repressive regimes that not only undermine the evolution of democracy, but they continue to engage in human rights abuses. Interestingly the threat of WMD in the region remains just that a threat. The war in Iraq represented a tool that was supposed to eliminate the threat, but there is evidence to the contrary. The nuclear production facilities scattered across Iran and the clandestine program in Syria (one that refused to permit IAEA inspections beyond the site bombed by Israel) are indicators of a continued problem (dramatically set back after an Israeli surgical strike destroyed the facility). Lastly, the search for a viable strategy to secure peace between the Israeli's and the Palestinians remains an opportunity unfilled. The continued silence on the future of the Golan Heights remains an impediment to peace between Israel and Syria. Then there is the matter of Islamic radicalism which undermines real and sustainable growth of democracy, and there is this supplemental dilemma: not only is terrorism a continuing threat in the region, but there are a host of terror safe havens in many states the region. The election of President Obama represents a clear repudiation of the assumptions that undergirded President Bush's strategy in the Middle East, but the realities of the Middle East represent a daunting challenge for the new administration.

OBAMA'S STATEMENTS ON THE MIDDLE EAST

Throughout the presidential campaign critics incessantly focused on Barack Obama's lack of experience in foreign policy. Many critics questioned how Obama would deal with the formidable problems that exist in the Middle East. Obama's response to critics that regularly spoke of the "experience factor" involved his efforts to articulate that he understood more about the region than he was given credit for. His most profound statement on his "Middle East principles" came not from a major foreign policy speech, but in the form of an article in *Foreign Affairs*. In the article Obama returned to an old refrain: Iraq. According to Obama, "The morass in Iraq has made it immeasurably harder to confront and work through the many other problems in the region—and it has made many of those problems considerably more dangerous. Changing the dynamic in Iraq will allow us to focus our attention and influence on resolving the festering conflict between the Israelis and the Palestinians—a task that the Bush administration neglected for years."[176]

Iraq of course is a dilemma that will not soon end. Indeed, it is certain that Iraq will remain a protracted problem until Obama meets his pledge to withdraw US troops from the country. Elsewhere in the article Obama unveils his vision for US foreign policy in the region.

> For more than three decades, Israelis, Palestinians, Arab leaders, and the rest of the world have looked to America to lead the effort to build the road to a lasting peace. In recent years, they have all too often looked in vain. Our starting point must always be a clear and strong commitment to the security of Israel, our strongest ally in the region and its only established democracy. That commitment is all the more important as we contend with growing threats in the region—a strengthened Iran, a chaotic Iraq, the resurgence of al Qaeda, [and] the reinvigoration of Hamas and Hezbollah. Now more than ever, we must strive to secure a lasting settlement of the conflict with two states living side by side in peace and security. To do so, we must help the Israelis identify and strengthen those partners who are truly committed to peace, while isolating those who seek conflict and instability. Sustained American leadership for peace and security will require patient effort and the personal commitment of the president of the United States. That is a commitment I will make. Throughout the Middle East, we must harness American power to reinvigorate American diplomacy. Tough-minded diplomacy backed by the whole range of instruments of American power—political, economic, and military—could bring success even when dealing with long-standing adversaries such as Iran and Syria. Our policy of issuing threats and relying on intermediaries to curb Iran's nuclear program, sponsorship of terrorism, and regional aggression is failing. Although we must not rule out using military force, we should not hesitate to talk directly to Iran. Our diplomacy should aim to raise the cost for Iran of continuing its nuclear program by applying tougher sanctions and increasing pressure from its key trading partners. The world must work to stop Iran's uranium-enrichment program and prevent Iran from acquiring nuclear weapons. It is far too dangerous to have nuclear weapons in the hands of a radical theocracy. At the same time, we must show Iran—and especially the Iranian people—what could be gained from fundamental change: economic engagement, security assurances, and diplomatic relations. Diplomacy combined with pressure could also reorient Syria away from its radical agenda to a more moderate stance—which could, in turn, help stabilize Iraq, isolate Iran, free Lebanon from Damascus' grip, and better secure Israel.[177]

Inside the foreign policy community there was little response to his vision. Many believed the article represented nothing more than an expanded version of his speech "America's Moment" that was delivered to Chicago Council on Global Affairs in April of 2007. With regard to the press, the coverage of the article in *Foreign Affairs* was muted.

Notwithstanding the absence of press coverage on the article, Obama's Middle East education continued to evolve during the course of the presidential campaign. In an interview with Fareed Zakaria on the *CNN* program GPS on July 13, 2008 Obama used the occasion to correct the record on his statement in support of the division of Jerusalem. Obama started his statement by acknowledging what he contended was nothing more than an inappropriate choice of words. According to Obama, "The point we were simply making was, is that we don't want barbed wire running through Jerusalem, similar to the way it was prior to the 1967 war, that it is possible for us to create a Jerusalem that is cohesive and coherent."[178]

On the controversial issue of negotiations with the Palestinians Obama made a number of significant statements. In late July of 2008 he noted that peace can only come if "…both sides on this equation … make some calculations. Israel may seek 1967-plus' and justify it in terms of the buffer that they need for security purposes. They've got to consider whether getting that buffer is worth the antagonism of the other party. The Palestinians are going to have to make a calculation: Are we going to fight for every inch of that 1967 border or, given the fact that 40 years have now passed, and new realities have taken place on the ground, do we take a deal that may not perfectly align with the 1967 boundaries? My sense is that both sides recognize that there's going to have to be some give. The question from my perspective is can the parties move beyond a rigid, formulaic or ideological approach and take a practical approach that looks at the larger picture and says, 'What's going to be the best way for us to achieve security and peace?'"[179]

In subsequent comments Obama made sure that his statements on whether Israel should abide by previous agreements were unequivocal: "I think that Israel should abide by previous agreements and commitments that have been made, and aggressive settlement construction would seem to violate the spirit at least, if not the letter, of agreements that have been made previously. Israel's security concerns, I think, have to be taken into account, via negotiation. I think the parties in previous discussions have stated that settlement construction doesn't necessarily contribute to that enhanced security. I think there are those who would argue that the more settlements there are, the more Israel has to invest in protecting those settlements and the more tensions arise that may undermine Israel's long-term security. Ultimately, though, these are part of the discussions that have to take place between the parties. But I think that, based on what's previously been said, for Israel to make sure that it is aligned with those previous statements is going to be helpful to the process."[180]

Barack Obama did not hide his criticism of the Bush administrations policies and how they affected the influence of Iran, Hezbollah and Hamas. The following statement is instructive: "I think there is no doubt that there is a connection between Iran's strengthening over the last couple of years, partly because some strategic errors have been made on the part of the West. And [the same goes for] the increasing boldness of Hezbollah and Hamas. But I don't think that's the only factor and criterion in the lack of progress. Hamas's victory in the [Palestinian Authority] election can partly be traced to a sense of frustration among the Palestinian people over how Fatah, over a relatively lengthy period of time, had failed to deliver basic services. I get a strong impression that [PA President Mahmoud] Abbas and [Prime Minister Salaam] Fayad are doing everything they can to address some of those systemic failures by the Palestinian Authority. The failures of Hamas in Gaza to deliver an improved quality of life for their people give pause to the Palestinians to think that pursuing that approach automatically assures greater benefits. You know, look, I arrive at this with no illusions as to the difficulty in terms of what is required. But I think it's important for us to keep working at it, frankly, because Israel's security and peace in the region depend on it."[181]

The issue of Middle East Peace assumed prominence during different periods of the presidential election, however, Obama's statements on Iran produced strong reactions from presidential candidates and from within the foreign policy community (this is true of his statements on Iraq, where he spoke of the "phased" withdrawal of American troops).

Obama subjected himself to criticism when he opined that diplomacy could be used as a mechanism for better relations with Iran, and perhaps ending its nuclear ambitions. In a *CNN/YouTube* Democrat Presidential Candidate Debate in Charleston, South Carolina on July 23, 2007, Obama was asked the following question: "[Would] you be willing to meet separately, without precondition, during the first year of your administration, in Washington or anywhere else, with the leaders of Iran, Syria, Venezuela, Cuba and North Korea, in order to bridge the gap that divides our countries?" His response was as follows: "I will meet with them—the leaders of hostile nations like Iran, Syria, Venezuela, Cuba, and North Korea, and the reason is this, the notion that somehow not talking to countries is punishment to them—which has been the guiding principle of this administration—is ridiculous."[182] The statement represented Obama's efforts to illustrate what he called a need for a new diplomacy and new leadership in US foreign policy.

As one would imagine, the response raised eyebrows and unleashed criticism. Senator Hillary Clinton called the statement "naïve" and symbolized Obama's inexperience in foreign affairs. Senator Joseph Biden called the statement the "wrong answer." Obama would make subsequent statements that were designed to clarify the earlier statement. On the Obama-Biden website, for example, under the heading of "new diplomacy," the statement read as follows: [Obama] "supports tough, direct presidential diplomacy with Iran without preconditions. Now is the time to pressure Iran directly to change their troubling behavior. Obama and Biden would offer the Iranian regime a choice. If Iran abandons its nuclear program and support for terrorism, we will offer incentives like membership in the World Trade Organization, economic investments, and a move toward normal diplomatic relations. If Iran continues its troubling behavior, we will step up our economic pressure and political isolation. Seeking this kind of comprehensive settlement with Iran is our best way to make progress."[183]

In recognition of the evolving criticism, allies of Barack Obama moved to reduce the damage caused by the initial and subsequent statements on meeting with rogue states without preconditions. Individuals that include the likes of Gary Hart, Chairman of the Democratic Leadership Conference (DLC), Harold Ford, Governor Bill Richardson, former Representative David Bonior, Senator Tom Daschle, and others, all raced to clarify Obama's statements. While each of the statements of support were interesting and designed to correct and refute criticism directed toward Obama, Tom Daschle's comments proved to have the most traction. Consider the exchange between *CNN*'s John Roberts and Daschle on *CNN*'s "America Morning" on May 20, 2008:

> **Daschle**: "I Would Not Say That We Would Meet Unconditionally—Of Course There Are Conditions ...." *CNN*'s **John Roberts**: "Senator, you thought about running for

the nomination in the 2004 election briefly. If you had become president, would you have met with Ahmadinejad and others without precondition in the first year of your presidency?" **Daschle**: "Well, I think it's important to emphasize again when we talk about precondition we're just saying everything needs to be on the table. I would not say that we would meet unconditionally—of course there are conditions that we would involve in preparation in getting ready for the diplomacy, but clearly, John, we've got to start talking. We have to start working through the differences we have, and of course I'd meet with them." **Roberts**: "But he clearly said, clearly agreed that he would meet without precondition." **Daschle**: "Well, without precondition simply means we wouldn't put obstacles in the way of discussing the differences between us. That's really what they're saying, what Barack is saying."[184]

In another example, the co-host of "Fox and Friends" Steve Doocy asked the following question to Governor Richardson on May 21, 2008: "Governor, doesn't Senator Obama want to talk to Ahmadinejad?" Richardson's response did not help Obama. The governors confusing response was as follows: "He [Obama] wants to talk to the Iranian leadership. He wants to talk to North Korea. But he wants diplomatic preparation before doing that with Cuba, look, this embargo hasn't worked. And what Obama is saying that let's talk to the Cuban leadership."[185]

In the wake of these statements of support, many in the foreign policy community questioned the approach and certainly the "unfortunate statements" made by Obama. Still there were those that wanted to give Obama a second look, and felt with direction there was a possibility that change could indeed come to the Middle East. The words of Stephen Zunes are telling: "Many are holding out hope that as president, Obama would be more progressive than he is letting on and that he would take bolder initiatives to shift US policy in the region further away from its current militaristic orientation than he may feel comfortable advocating as a candidate. Indeed, given how even the hawkish John Kerry was savaged by the right-wing over his positions on Middle East security issues during his campaign for the presidency, the threat of such attacks could be enough to have given Senator Obama pause in making more direct challenges to the status quo as a candidate. But he could be open to more rational and creative approaches to the Middle East once in office."[186]

CONFLICT OVER MIDDLE EAST PEACE DIRECTIONS

As noted above during the presidential campaign Obama made a host of statements about Middle East Peace, Iran and Iraq. Now in office what remains problematic is how the Obama administration would confront radical Islam and the ongoing threat of terrorism in the region. There is a dilemma: Obama has yet to define a clear strategy that defines his administration framework for Middle East Peace.

During the campaign and in the earlier period of the administration, quietly a bureaucratic struggle for the direction of Middle East policy continues. In many ways the internal struggle is consistent with all administrations. The issue of consequence is how the internal power struggle will determine the direction of policy. Throughout the campaign Obama informed the world that he intended to press for an agreement in Middle East. One thing is certain Obama has a wealth of regional experts that will be helpful in any attempt to secure an agreement. Quietly since the campaign and long after election of President Barack Obama a struggle is underway for the control of US policy in region. The individuals at the heart of this struggle are former Clinton administration envoy Dennis Ross and Daniel Kurtzer, who served in the position of US Ambassador to Israel during the administration of George W. Bush. Reports suggest that acrimony impaired the relationship between Ross and Kurtzer. In an example of the problems between the two many assert that Kurtzer's statement that Ross is "tilted" toward the Israeli side, and worse, that he "listened to what Israel wanted and then tried to sell it toward the Arabs," questioned the veracity of Ross is central to animosity between the two men.

This statement, notwithstanding, both individuals were central nodes of the Obama policy team during the campaign that was decidedly pro-Israel. The difference is a matter of degrees—and not very many degrees—within a firmly pro-Israel policy team, and there are no obvious differences of policy between the two men. Ross, the supposed man of the right, was central to the Oslo peace accords and is disliked by some conservatives in Israel and the United States; Kurtzer is considered by many to be one the critical advisors to President Bush on the Middle East. The differences between the two experts have been described this way: "Kurtzer emerged in the Democratic primary as an ambassador to the pro-Israel and Jewish communities for Obama. Ross, a trusted figure among relatively hawkish American Jewish leaders, advised both Obama and Clinton in the primary, and was a behind the scenes force in the general election, assuring figures such as *New York Daily News* publisher Mort Zuckerman that Obama was committed to Israel's safety. Obama has worked to keep both men inside the tent. They served together on his Middle East transition team, along with Biden adviser Tony Blinken and two campaign aides, Dan Shapiro and Eric Lynn. But camps have begun to develop: The liberal Israeli newspaper *Haaretz* floated Kurtzer as "special Mideast envoy." A Kurtzer admirer in Obama's camp said choosing him would send the message that "we want to draw on the past, but we want to move forward on our own and not be bound by that. Meanwhile, critics say Kurtzer lacks Ross's stature, and that his relationship as ambassador with the icon of the Israeli center-right, then-Prime Minister Ariel Sharon, left something to be desired. They see Ross in a more senior policy making role than envoy, if there even is an envoy."[187]

The debate which emerged during the presidential campaign and continued well into the transition period but dissipated quietly once President Obama made the decision to select Dennis Ross as Secretary of State Hillary Clinton's Special Advisor for The Gulf and Southwest Asia (George Mitchell was appointed to the position of US Middle East Envoy). For his part Daniel Kurtzer, who lost his bid to become Middle East Envoy, accepted the position of Professor of Middle Eastern Studies at Princeton University. In the final analysis critics charge the Middle Eastern team is hardly new and is devoid of a new ideas or a new framework to push for the next phase of peace in the region.

The aforementioned perspective gives the impression that the dispute over the course and direction of Middle East Peace is entirely among diplomats within the Obama administration. The reality is the conflict is far more pervasion. The other variables (which include elements on NSA staff, the CIA, those among Central Command, and other components of the foreign policy bureaucracy) are equally important in determining the outcome of the internal conflict, and ultimately the course and direction of US Middle East strategy. One thing that is emerging is there is a clear distinction between the internal conflict that occurred under the Bush administration and what is currently unfolding in the Obama administration.

During the Bush administration, the State Department was the source of every call for envoys, roadmaps, summits, and efforts to revive the peace process. And for most of the Bush era, these calls were rejected by the White House and Pentagon—which believed that the Israeli-Palestinian struggle was a symptom of deeper pathologies within the Islamic and Arab world, and not the underlying cause of Middle Eastern terrorism. Within the Obama administration, this dynamic is likely to be reversed. It may be the White House—and, more specifically, the likely national security advisor, James Jones—that will be the passionate proponent of peace processing. Or, as he told the newsletter *Inside the Pentagon* last month, "Nothing is more important" to regional security in the Middle East than resolving the Israeli-Palestinian conflict. Jones, the retired commandant of the Marine Corps, has significant experience in the Middle East. Last November, Condoleezza Rice appointed him as her special envoy for Middle East security, with a particular emphasis on working with the Israel Defense Forces (IDF) and Palestinian security services. Last August, he drafted a report on security in the Palestinian territories that is said to have been highly critical of Israel's policies in the territories and its attitude toward the Palestinian Authority's security services. The White House and State Department opted not to publish the report.[188]

What we may be seeing is a return to "active" and "strong" national security advisor. The absence of an active and strong national security advisor significantly affected policy making during the Bush years. This void was filled by Vice President Cheney, which reduced the authority of Colin Powell over at State, and undermined Rice's authority during her tenure as national security advisor. It will be interesting to watch the Hillary-Clinton-James Jones dynamic. There is little doubt that this will be a critical issue for determining long term Middle East strategy. Finally, there is another variable that will be important: the still undefined portfolio of Vice President Joseph Biden. Given his foreign policy credentials one should anticipate that he will seek an active role on the formation of administration Middle East Peace policy.

In the end there is a strong likelihood that Obama's Middle East strategy will closely mirror President Clinton's. What accounts for this assertion? Before providing evidence in support of the above supposition it is important to briefly outline the differences between the two presidential approaches.

There are some critical differences in the Clinton and Obama approaches. Because the United States is confronting two wars, and with the economy in the worst shape in decades, Obama faces the reality that Middle East Peace is not likely to be a high priority on the presidential agenda during the first year of his presidency. Clinton did not have to contend with such issues. That is the end of the Cold War and the "peace dividend" made it easier for Clinton to pick and choose which foreign policy issues to tackle. Additionally, though Clinton played no role in the Oslo Accord, he did bring the participants to Washington, D.C. for a signing ceremony. Thus the agreement gave Clinton instantaneous credibility even he did nothing to bring about the agreement. Obama will not be afforded such an advantage. He will have to obtain credibility the old fashioned way: he will earn it. His appearance on the Arab satellite station *Al Arabiya* notwithstanding while the interview was an important first step but it had little to do with the policy but had more to do with public relations. The interview and the president's words were well received but like all previous US leaders Obama will be judged on his policy, or lack thereof in the region. Unfortunately, the president continues to make bold speeches, such as his address in June 4, 2009 in Cairo, Egypt which fulfilled his campaign promise. While the speech is clearly a change in the tone of US policy toward the Muslim World it will take the entire course of the Obama administration before we can discern if it truly impacted overall US Middle East strategy.

There are other points of departure. To begin with Obama made statements that indicate his policies will include components that were not considered or introduced by Clinton. During the campaign Obama promised negotiations with Iran and other countries without preconditions. Even though the language of his statements on the subject changed, due to criticism that he was naïve, the basic objective calling for negotiations with Iran remains constant. Second, Obama called for direct talks with Syria, another major departure from Clinton. In the interview with the *Jerusalem Post* on July 24, 2008 Obama made the following statement: "My general view is that initiating direct contacts between the United States and other countries is a generally smart practice—if nothing else just to get better intelligence on what they are thinking, on what their approaches are, what their calculations are, what their interests are. I think that based on conversations I've had here in Israel as well as conversations with leaders elsewhere in the region, there is the possibility at least that the Syrian government genuinely seeks to break out of the isolation. What price they are willing to pay to break out of that isolation, is an unanswered question. It's worth exploring. And if in fact there are some genuine signals that Syria is willing to drive out terrorists in their midst, shut down the arms flow into Lebanon, or to otherwise engage in more responsible behavior, I think it could be a shift in the region that would be extremely advantageous. And the United States should partner with Israel as well as moderate forces in the Palestinian community to pursue that."[189]

The objectives of such talks, according to Obama, could produce a series of benefits. Equally important the Obama administration would pursue such talks with a clear set of objectives: "I would engage Syria in direct bilateral talks. We should insist on our core demands: cooperation in stabilizing Iraq; ending support for terrorist groups that threaten Israel; and respect for Lebanon's sovereignty and independence. We should make plain there are two paths ahead: greater engagement, improved political ties and economic cooperation or greater isolation through imposition of the full range of sanctions in the Syria Accountability Act which will make it difficult for companies and financial institutions that do business in Syria to continue to do business in the US. In this process, we should work closely with our European partners; incentives and disincentives will be far more effective if the EU is on board."[190]

Like Clinton, Obama campaigned on the importance of Middle East Peace. Second, the most obvious indicator of the continuance of the Clinton administration approach is the number of former Clinton Middle East officials that are now serving with the Obama administration. Third, as pointed out earlier Dennis Ross is now serving as special envoy, a position he formerly held during the Clinton administration. Fourth, the Obama and Clinton administrations are linked by two additional realities: both are domestic president's whose mandate involved the economy; and second, each Democratic president, in the area of foreign policy, was deemed inexperienced. Interesting both viewed the Middle East as the place to expend political capital, viewing the region as the best location to maximize political benefits. Fifth, each had to contend with the intractable problem of Iraq. Clinton launched several surgical strikes to force Saddam

Hussein to comply with United Nations sanctions. Obama on the other hand is attempting to end the US occupation of Iraq. Though each president approached the problem of Iraq from different perspectives, there is a central linkage: no review of Middle East policy can commence without serious attention to Iraq.

Sixth, both Clinton and Obama have another commonality with regard to Middle East Peace: boldness without a grand strategy. The repeated efforts by Clinton to build confidence building measures, along with his all-too-numerous efforts to conduct personal diplomacy, along with the bold approach to tackle the always controversial question of the future of Jerusalem, and the "eleventh hour diplomacy" represented the former president's bid to secure an agreement before he left office collectively demonstrate the expansive nature of Clinton's Middle Peace policies. As noted above, beginning with his campaign statements and the early period of his administration, Obama's approach to the region is also marked by an expansive Middle East policy. Attempts to open new diplomatic fronts in Iran and Syria, and to lesser degree, Lebanon, are clear indicators that Obama's agenda is far more expansive than that of Clinton and Bush. But Obama does not want to stop there; his agenda includes the withdrawal of American forces from Iraq, and additionally, dealing with Iran's pursuit of nuclear weapons.

While boldness may be attached to both presidential Middle East policies, they are linked in another way: both presidents lacked a grand strategy for the region. The involvement of Clinton and Obama, despite the expansive nature of their policies, is consistent with the policies of all US presidents from Richard Nixon to the current occupant of the White House: each of the presidential policies is governed by "reactive engagement." According to Steve A. Yetiv reactive engagement "reveals that the United States clearly exhibited significantly shifting, improvised, and reactive policies that were responses to unanticipated and unpredictable events and threats."[191] Republican reactive engagement is governed by pragmatic realism during the Nixon and George H.W. Bush administrations, and a neoconservative impulse that governed Middle Eastern diplomacy under George W. Bush. With respect to Democratic presidents, reactive engagement is problematic because their policies in the region are driven by "wrong headed idealism" that induces "high minded optimism" but other than President Carter's Camp David agreement there have been no other signature accomplishments. This is true of Clinton and given that Obama has made a host of statements without a clear plan, it is suspected that there is unlikely to be a major agreement under the current president.

If President Obama is to succeed in the region he would do well to remember the words of Kenneth Pollack, who asserts in his book that *A Path Out of the Desert: A Grand Strategy for America in the Middle East* "An overarching conception of what it is that we seek to achieve, how we intend to do it and how to employ the full panoply of foreign policy tools." Obama can not have a grand strategy and therefore a chance for success in the region without a clear set of achievable objectives, and recognition of the instruments that are required for their implementation. Thus uttering such words as he did on trip to Middle East in July of 2008 "I'm here on this trip to reaffirm the special relationship between Israel and the United States, my abiding commitment to its security, and my hope that I can serve as an effective partner, whether as a ... senator or as a president, in bringing about a more lasting peace in the region"[192] may make for a great sound bite but are not the basis for a sound policy or grand strategy.

The crisis in the Gaza beginning in December 2008 and continuing in January of 2009 is symbolic of the failure of the United States to have a grand strategy. The Bush administration, and Obama's key advisors, quietly hoped that Israeli Defense Forces would greatly reduce if not destroy Hamas altogether. Neither appeared to ask the strategic question: How do you rebuild confidence building measures in the wake of a cease fire? Even with Hamas badly battered, Palestinians remain sympathetic to the terrorist group. Equally important the Palestinian leadership will remain governed by divided loyalties—Hamas and Fatah—making it difficult to implement negotiations toward a two-state solution. President Obama can not begin any meaningful diplomacy so long as the Palestinian civil war continues. President Obama, Secretary of State Hillary Clinton and administration Middle East advisors should carefully consider and then implement a workable grand strategy for the region. Perhaps President Obama may succeed in negotiations where Bush and Clinton failed.

CHAPTER 7
RETHINKING THE WAR ON TERROR

Candidate Obama sent shock waves through the national security establishment when he opined that terrorism should be treated "like a law enforcement problem." This issue arose in the wake of a Supreme Court decision that extended rights to detainees in Guantanamo Bay detention facilities to challenge their incarceration in federal court. In an extended response to the Supreme Court decision, in an interview with *ABC* news Obama made the following comment: "What we know is that, in previous terrorist attacks, for example, the first attack against the World Trade Center, we were able to arrest those responsible, put them on trial. They are currently in US prisons, incapacitated.... And the fact that the administration has not tried to do that has created a situation where not only have we never actually put many of these folks on trial, but we have destroyed our credibility when it comes to rule of law all around the world, and given a huge boost to terrorist recruitment in countries that say, 'Look, this is how the United States treats Muslims.' So that, I think, is an example of something that was unnecessary. We could have done the exact same thing, but done it in a way that was consistent with our laws."[193]

As one would anticipate the Republicans blasted the statement. Former New York City Mayor Rudolf Giuliani observed, "Throughout this campaign, I have been very concerned that the Democrats want to take a step back to the failed policies that treated terrorism solely as a law enforcement matter rather than a clear and present danger. Barack Obama appears to believe that terrorists should be treated like criminals—a belief that underscores his fundamental lack of judgment regarding our national security. In a post 9/11 world, we need to remain on offense against the terrorist threat which seeks to destroy our very way of life. We need a leader like John McCain who has the experience and judgment necessary to protect the American people."[194] The most piquant criticism was authored by Randy Scheunemann the campaign foreign policy advisor for Senator John McCain, who said the following:

> Barack Obama's belief that we should treat terrorists as nothing more than common criminals demonstrates a stunning and alarming misunderstanding of the threat we face from radical Islamic extremism. Obama holds up the prosecution of the terrorists who bombed the World Trade Center in 1993 as a model for his administration, when in fact this failed approach of treating terrorism simply as a matter of law enforcement rather than a clear and present danger to the United States contributed to the tragedy of

September 11th. This is change that will take us back to the failed policies of the past and every American should find this mindset troubling.[195]

These and other statements produced a similar refrain: That Barack Obama, if he were to become commander-in-chief, viewed US strategy against terrorism through a pre-September 11 prism.

After criticism that his statement represented a possible return to Clinton's failed approach to fighting terrorism, Obama settled on an "old statement" that became more defensible: "We must forge a more effective global response to the terrorism that came to our shores on an unprecedented scale on 9/11."[196] Following questions about the absence of a defined strategy Obama issued a statement designed to illustrate his competence on this critical campaign issue: "We must refocus our efforts on Afghanistan and Pakistan—the central front in our war against al Qaeda—so that we are confronting terrorists where their roots run deepest."[197] Evidence presented in this chapter demonstrates the president will have a relatively short period to pursue Al Qaeda in the vast lawless regions of Pakistan and to increase the American troop presence to confront the ever-expanding Taliban threat in Afghanistan. Both initiatives will require patience and direct presidential involvement. At another level this chapter demonstrates that Obama will repeat a critical miscalculation of the Bush administration: the failure to fight the war on terror in clearly defined phases. It is argued herein that President Obama's most enduring foreign policy legacy will develop during his stewardship of the war on terror.

BUSH AND THE WAR ON TERROR:

Well into the Obama administration there is one thing the president has discovered: other than the foolish decision to invade Iraq President Bush created and implemented an impressive grand strategy to conduct the war on terror. The "four pronged" components quickly developed into the center of gravity of President Bush's strategy.

To understand the aforementioned core elements of the former president's strategy it is important to remember that they were not created by the Bush administration. Rather, in an odd irony, an administration that spoke of "ABC" (Anything But Clinton)—a reference that indicated a strong objection to following any of Clinton's policies—the four components of Bush's grand strategy mirrored the Clinton version. The first component involved the employment of diplomacy, which entailed the construction of a "grand coalition" that would be arrayed against transnational terrorism. The second component involved the unprecedented international cooperation designed to obstruct and eventually prohibit the flow of funds to al Qaeda and its affiliated groups; the same coalition would be prepared to mount a diplomatic offensive should the need arise. The funding sources to Al Qaeda and other terrorists groups were not entirely disrupted, but President Bush and the international coalition succeeded in making great strides in this area. Third, this component called for the coordination of international law enforcement and intelligence services to seek out and prosecute terrorists, and where ever possible prevent future terrorist attacks. This strategy is the least discussed component, but it is by far one of the more successful aspects of the strategy. To validate this point consider there is not a day when multiple countries are sharing information to thwart a terrorist attack or a state or multiple states providing information that led to the capture or killing of a terrorist. Fourth, this component requires the use of force as the critical factor in achieving the long-range objective of eradicating international terrorism.[198] This component required the successful deployment of military power all over the globe. This component did have a major setback: the misapplication of force in Iraq. Beyond this egregious misstep, this component, like the other three components, proved invaluable to President Bush's efforts to confront international terrorism.

As critical as the aforementioned components may be they do not begin to tell the story of the complexity of President Bush's strategy. In the second layer, as corollaries to its first layer, the administration offered these supplemental instruments to "disrupt and destroy terrorist organizations by":

- Direct and continuous action... [with the] immediate focus [on] terrorist organizations of global reach and any terrorist or state sponsor of terrorism which attempts to gain or use weapons of mass destruction or their precursors;
- While the United States will constantly strive to enlist the support of the international community, we will not hesitate to act alone, if necessary exercise our right to prevent them from doing harm against our people and our country; and,
- Denying further sponsorship, support, and sanctuary to terrorists by convincing or compelling states to accept their sovereign responsibilities.
- The administration also announced "we will also wage a war of ideas to win the battle against international terrorism." This includes:
- Using the full influence of the United States, and working closely with allies and friends, to make clear that all acts of terrorism will be viewed in the same light as slavery, piracy, or genocide: behavior that no respectable government can condone or support and all must oppose;
- Supporting moderate and modern governments, especially in the Muslim world, to ensure that the conditions and ideologies that promote terrorism do not find fertile ground in any nation;
- Diminishing the underlying conditions that spawn terrorism by enlisting the international community to focus its efforts and resources on areas most at risk, and using effective public diplomacy to promote the free flow of information and ideas to kindle the hopes and aspirations of global terrorism.[199]

This second layer is indicative of the Bush administrations' efforts to ensure a global response to transnational terrorism. Similarly, the *2002 National Security Strategy of the United States* operationalized and provided a "sense of mission" for critical elements of the national security bureaucracy (CIA, Defense Department, State Department, FBI, etc.). The document is as close as we may see to the historic NSC-68 presidential directive. Equally important Bush created two additional layers to preclude future terrorist attacks on the continental United States. The first was the creation of United States Northern Command (USNORTCOM) whose mission is to "provide command and control of Department of Defense (DoD) homeland defense efforts and to coordinate defense support of civil authorities." Since its inception in October of 2002 USNORTHCOM successfully prevented any post-9/11 attacks. The second was the creation of the Department of Homeland Security. The new department's central emphasis involved the coordination of information sharing of a host of executive institutions with responsibility for protecting the continental United States.

President Bush's grand strategy included efforts to contend with terrorism in specific regions. In its focus on Africa, no region, other than the Middle East, received so much attention from the US Government. In the administrations strategic calculus they identified that Africa would be a likely focus of Al Qaeda once the American military targeted the networks central safe haven and operational base in Afghanistan. To that end the Bush administration feared that the network would set up bases in Somalia, Sudan and elsewhere on the continent. In the administrations war councils a decision was made: President Bush decided to create two major coalitions, The Combined Joint Task Force in the Horn of Africa (CJTF-HOA) and the Pan Sahel Initiative (PSI) later to be replaced by the more successful Trans-Sahara Counterterrorism Initiative (TSCTI). These organizations have transformed the counterterrorism capabilities of member states. Similarly, the coalition partnerships have not only increased the training capabilities of their troops, but the same member states of the aforementioned organizations have successfully adapted to military-to-military contact of regional states, and the coalitions will impact the militaries of participant states long after the threat of terror has subsided. There was another significant creation—the creation of African Military Command (AFRICOM)—that will be used as a long term tool for the purpose of counterterrorism and to advance US interests in the region. Not only is AFRICOM needed (it ended the need to have three regional military organizations—European Command, Pacific Command and Central Command)—from the perspective of American military, but the organization will assist in confronting the long term commitment to the evolving security needs in Africa.[200]

OBAMA'S STATEMENTS ON THE WAR ON TERROR

Any criticism of the war on terror begins with the decision to shift focus from Afghanistan to Iraq. Barack Obama articulated this point whenever the opportunity arose. In his book the *Audacity of Hope* Obama launched one of his strongest assessments of Bush's unpopular decision to shift to Iraq before the postwar reconstruction process had concluded in Afghanistan. According to Obama, "The struggle against Islamic-based terrorism will be not simply be a military campaign but a battle for public opinion in the Islamic world, among our allies and in the US. Osama bin Laden understands that he cannot defeat the US in a conventional war. What he and his allies can do is inflict enough pain to provoke a reaction of the sort we've seen in Iraq—a botched and ill-advised US military incursion into a Muslim country, which in turn spurs on insurgencies based on religious sentiment and nationalist pride, which in turn necessitates a lengthy and difficult US occupation. All of this fans anti-American sentiment among Muslims, and increases the pool of potential terrorist recruits. That's the plan for winning a war from a cave, and so far, we are playing to script. To change that script, we'll need to make sure that any exercise of American military power helps rather than hinders our broader goals: to incapacitate the destructive potential of terrorist networks *and* win this global battle of ideas."[201]

In his critique of Senate passage of S. 3930 Military Commissions Act of 2006 which approved US torture of detainees and strips Constitutional rights away from detainees, Obama made the following statement: "We have Al Qaeda and the Taliban regrouping in Afghanistan while we look the other way. We have a war in Iraq that our own government's intelligence says is serving as Al Qaeda's best recruitment tool. And we have recommendations from the bipartisan 9/11 commission that we still refuse to implement five years after the fact.... This is not how a serious Administration would approach the problem of terrorism."[202]

Obama seized on the opportunity to attack what he believed was the source of the administrations decision to shift away from Afghanistan and then attack Iraq. According to Obama, "part of the reason that we neglected Afghanistan, part of the reason that we didn't go after bin Laden as aggressively as we should have is we were distracted by a war of choice. That's the flaw of the Bush doctrine. It wasn't that he went after those who attacked America. It was that he went after those who didn't. As a consequence, we have been bogged down, paid extraordinary—an extraordinary price in blood and treasure…."[203]

Throughout the presidential campaign Obama was fixated on Afghanistan and Pakistan. In "Renewing American Leadership" Obama made a series of statements to buttress his contention that these two states are essential to winning the global war on terror.

> We must refocus our efforts on Afghanistan and Pakistan—the central front in our war against al Qaeda—so that we are confronting terrorists where their roots run deepest. Success in Afghanistan is still possible, but only if we act quickly, judiciously, and decisively. We should pursue an integrated strategy that reinforces our troops in Afghanistan and works to remove the limitations placed by some NATO allies on their forces. Our strategy must also include sustained diplomacy to isolate the Taliban and more effective development programs that target aid to areas where the Taliban are making inroads. I will join with our allies in insisting—not simply requesting—that Pakistan crack down on the Taliban, pursue Osama bin Laden and his lieutenants, and end its relationship with all terrorist groups. At the same time, I will encourage dialogue between Pakistan and India to work toward resolving their dispute over Kashmir and between Afghanistan and Pakistan to resolve their historic differences and develop the Pashtun border region. If Pakistan can look toward the east with greater confidence, it will be less likely to believe that its interests are best advanced through cooperation with the Taliban.[204]

These statements by themselves do not come close to expressing the expansive views articulated by Obama. To demonstrate the positions made by Obama on Afghanistan and Pakistan it is essential to examine them—separately—despite the fact that Obama and his advisors have repeatedly tried to link them.

As is always the case with the views of a presidential candidate: such views undergo a transformation over time. This evolution occurs for a number of reasons. The obvious is that a candidate may make a controversial statement and thereafter goes through a period of damage control. Second, the candidate, as the campaign moves forward, becomes far more knowledgeable about a foreign policy issue and often becomes more descriptive in his/her explanations. Third, the nature of the question, particularly if it is specific, forces the candidate to provide a more substantive answer. Whether on Afghanistan or Pakistan, Obama's responses relative to both countries are consistent with the process.

Obama's early statements about the significance of Afghanistan to the war on terror were not always consistent, and were at times confusing. In a senate campaign debate with Alan Keyes on October 12, 2004 Obama made the following statement: "I have always thought that we did the right thing in Afghanistan. My only concern with respect to Afghanistan was that we diverted our attention from Afghanistan in terms of moving into Iraq and I think we could have done a better job of stabilizing that country than we have in providing assistance to the Afghani people."[205]

In a debate at Saint Anselm College on June 3, 2007 Obama demonstrated the significance of Afghanistan to resurrecting the war on terror and to eliminating future threats to homeland. According to Obama, "One of the things that I think is critical, as the next president, [is]… to make absolutely certain that we not only phase out the Iraq but we also focus on the critical battle that we have in Afghanistan and root out al Qaeda. If we do not do that, then we're going to potentially see another attack here in the US.[206]

Beginning with the Tim Russert interview on the *NBC* program "Meet the Press" on May 4, 2008 Obama's views became more specific and more indicative of the likely policies that he would pursue once he became president. Here is an exchange between Obama and Russert:

> **Russert**: The situation in Afghanistan is deteriorating as the Taliban continues to reconstitute itself. Would you, as president, be willing to have a military surge in Afghanistan in order to, once and for all, eliminate the Taliban? **Obama:** Yes. I think that's what we need. I think we need more troops there, I think we need to do a better job of reconstruction there. I think we have to be focused on Afghanistan. It is one of the reasons that I was opposed to the war in Iraq in the first place. We now know that Al Qaeda is stronger than any time since 2001. They are growing in capability. That is something that we've got to address. And we're also going to have to address the situation in Pakistan, where we now have, in the federated areas, Al Qaeda and the Taliban setting up bases there. We now have a new government in Pakistan. We have an opportunity to initiate a new relationship, so that we can get better cooperation to hunt down al Qaeda and make sure that that does not become a safe haven for them.[207]

In the first leg of his foreign tour that was designed to expand his foreign policy credentials Obama visited Afghanistan on July 21, 2008. A far more serious and statesman-like Obama warned the situation in Afghanistan is "urgent." Obama's speech represented a major policy statement that was designed to clarify his position on Afghanistan: "The Afghan government needs to do more. But we have to understand that the situation is precarious and urgent here in Afghanistan. And I believe this has to be our central focus, the central front, on our battle against terrorism. I think one of the biggest mistakes we've made strategically after 9/11 was to fail to finish the job here, focus our attention here. For at least a year now, I have called for two additional brigades, perhaps three. I think it's very important that we unify command more effectively to coordinate our military activities. But military alone is not going to be enough."[208]

Obama's statements in of themselves were not revealing. That is anyone with any knowledge of events in Afghanistan long ago recognized the need for a "new strategy," one that called for an increase in US troops. Indeed a troop increase had been underway, albeit at far lower levels, long before Obama made the decision to call upon President Bush to refocus the administrations attention on Afghanistan. The request for an increase in US troop commitments aside Obama, and his predecessor President Bush, were unable to increase NATO commitments. In fact the reality is most NATO contingents are involved in either decreasing their troops or removing them from Afghanistan altogether.

In the opening Democratic Primary debate in Iowa on August 19, 2007 Obama found himself embroiled in a major controversy. The issue debated by the Democratic presidential contenders involved whether the United States should use nuclear weapons to destroy Al Qaeda's safe haven in Pakistan. Here is an exchange that took place between Senator Hillary Clinton and Senator Obama. The Moderator George Stephanopoulos questioned Senator Clinton: [to Clinton]: You criticized Senator Obama for ruling out the use of nuclear weapons against Al Qaeda in Pakistan, yet you said the same against Bush's use of tactical nuclear weapons in Iran, saying: "I would certainly take nuclear weapons off the table." What's the difference there? Senator Clinton responded to the question this way: "I was asked specifically about the Bush-Cheney administration's policy to drum up support for military action against Iran. Combine that with their continuing effort to try to get "bunker-buster" nuclear bombs that could penetrate into the earth to go after deeply buried nuclear sites. This was not a hypothetical; this was a brush back against this administration which has been reckless and provocative." Stephanopoulos then shifted his focus to Obama: "Do you accept that distinction?" Obama's retort was as follows: "There was no difference. It is not hypothetical that Al Qaeda has established base camps in the hills between Afghanistan and Pakistan. No military expert would advise that we use nuclear weapons to deal with them, but we do have to deal with that problem."[209]

What escaped debate in the media is the reality that presidential candidates were involved in a heated discussion to use of nuclear weapons to deal with the world's number terrorist threat: Al Qaeda. Perhaps of greater consequence no one, the moderator or the candidates, seemed to understand or consider what the affect that any use of nuclear weapons would have on the people of Pakistan. Similarly, it appeared that none of the presidential candidates, particularly Obama and Clinton, recognized that their answers, for or against the use of nuclear weapons against al Qaeda, demonstrated the contempt they had for Pakistan's sovereignty and a sense of the feelings about Pakistan as an ally in the war on terror. It is this benign criticism that most certainly ruffled the feathers of a central ally in the war on terrorism.

In contrast Barack Obama's statement about taking some form of military operation in Pakistan given the right intelligence was far more controversial and represented a major departure from President Bush's policy. To provide some background consider that in December of 2005, President Bush, after receiving the advice of senior national security officials, canceled a military mission that would have targeted senior members of al Qaeda's leadership that included Osama bin Laden and his deputy Ayman al-Zawahri that were meeting in Pakistan's tribal region. In a speech delivered at the Woodrow Wilson International Center for Scholars in Washington, D.C., August 1, 2007 Obama announced a decision, oddly, that was clearly unilateral and consistent with the Bush Doctrine: "I understand that President Musharraf has his own challenges, but let me make this clear. There are terrorists holed up in those mountains who murdered 3,000 Americans. They are plotting to strike again. It was a terrible mistake to fail to act when we had a chance to take out an al Qaeda leadership meeting in 2005. If we have actionable intelligence about high-value terrorist targets and President Musharraf won't act, we will."[210]

In a subsequent primary debate in August of 2007 Obama attempted to step back from the criticism of his earlier statement. He remarked that "I did not say that we would immediately go in unilaterally. What I said was that we have to work with [Pakistan's President Pervez] Musharraf because the biggest threat to American security right now are in the northwest provinces of Pakistan and that we should continue to give him military aid contingent on him doing something about that."[211] This attempt represented the first of many transformations that only increased criticism and debate about the original statement.

In a subsequent presidential primary debate in January of 2008 Obama appeared to reverse himself. The moderator asked the following question, "You said back in August you would go into western Pakistan if you had actionable intelligence to go after it, whether or not the Pakistani government agreed. Do you stand by that?" Barack Obama's response was telling: "I absolutely do stand by it. We should do everything in our power to push and cooperate with the Pakistani government in taking on Al Qaeda, which is now based in northwest Pakistan. And what we know from our national intelligence estimates is that Al Qaeda is stronger now than at any time since 2001. And so, back in August, I said we should work with the Pakistani government, first of all to encourage democracy in Pakistan so you've got a legitimate government, and secondly that we have to press them to do more to take on Al Qaeda in their territory; and if they could not or would not do so, and we had actionable intelligence, then I would strike. The two heads of the 9/11 Commission a few months later wrote an editorial saying the exact same thing. I think it's indisputable that that should be our course."[212]

During the Presidential Debate with Senator John McCain on October 21, 2008 Obama was asked to respond to the following query: "Should the US respect Pakistani sovereignty and not pursue al Qaeda terrorists who maintain bases there?" After a brief pause to gather his thoughts Obama offered this detailed reply: "We have a difficult situation in Pakistan. I believe that part of the reason we have a difficult situation is because we made a bad judgment going into Iraq, when we hadn't finished the job of hunting down bin Laden and crushing al Qaeda. We have to change our policies with Pakistan. We can't coddle, as we did, a dictator, give him billions of dollars and then he's making peace treaties with the Taliban and militants. We're going to encourage Democracy in Pakistan, expand our non-military aid to Pakistan so that they have more of a stake in working with us, but insisting that they go after these militants. And if we have Osama bin Laden in our sights and the Pakistani government is unable or unwilling to take them out, then I think that we have to act and we will take them out. We will kill bin Laden; we will crush Al Qaeda. That has to be our biggest national security priority."[213]

In this version Obama omitted words that were clearly controversial. The aforementioned statement does not include troubling words like "unilateral" or this extended statement: "If we have actionable intelligence about high-value terrorist targets and President Musharraf won't act, we will." Having backed away from his original speech on August 1, 2007 an obvious question begs: what is Obama's "real position" in the event that military action is required against al Qaeda in Pakistan?

OPPORTUNITIES AND DILEMMAS FOR OBAMA IN THE CONDUCT OF THE WAR ON TERROR

The first year of Obama's presidency offers a wealth of opportunities and dilemmas to conduct the war on terror. Initially, he has the opportunity to meet his campaign pledge to "refocus our efforts on Afghanistan and Pakistan—the central front in our war against al Qaeda—so that we are confronting terrorists where their roots run deepest."[214] However, as mentioned above, President Bush has assisted President Obama in that he proposed an increase of 30,000 US troops into Afghanistan. Unfortunately the vast majority of those troops will not be in place until late in the summer of 2009. There is a second dilemma, "Afghanistan presents a unique set of problems: a rural-based insurgency, an enemy sanctuary in neighboring Pakistan, the chronic weakness of the Afghan government, a thriving narcotics trade, poorly developed infrastructure, and forbidding terrain."[215] In other words the realities in Afghanistan will require that Barack

Obama make Afghanistan a high priority and that he should be directly involved to ensure a sustained commitment.

There is a second verity that President Obama will have to accept. Back in the presidential campaign Obama argued "Success in Afghanistan is still possible, but only if we act quickly, judiciously, and decisively. We should pursue an integrated strategy that reinforces our troops in Afghanistan and works to remove the limitations placed by some NATO allies on their forces. Our strategy must also include sustained diplomacy to isolate the Taliban and more effective development programs that target aid to areas where the Taliban are making inroads."[216] The diplomatic track is a fantasy. Diplomacy is central to sustaining a relationship with Pakistan, and ending cross border Taliban and Al Qaeda insurgent attacks. But any diplomacy between Afghanistan and Pakistan will take months and perhaps years to cure a relationship that will have to overcome Afghan President Hamid Kharzai's distrust of the Pakistani government, particularly the ISI, which has repeatedly supported their Pashtun allies' efforts to undermine the government in Afghanistan.

Third, regardless of the increase in US forces, unless and until Afghan forces are capable of taking the fight to the Taliban or Al Qaeda, the hope of putting "an Afghan face on the counterinsurgency strategy" is a long term proposition. Then there is this issue: decreasing the insurgent-inspired attacks against the Afghan population and coalition troops. Utilizing the lessons of Iraq, it will take a year-plus to reverse the current trend where the Taliban is winning the critical "battle of hearts and minds." Similarly, given that this is a rural insurgency based in Pakistan, it is unclear how long it may take to contain and hopefully defeat the Taliban and al Qaeda.

Finally, there is this issue: sustaining attention in Afghanistan while remaining focused on dealing with Obama's central mandate, fixing the American economy. The need to pass legislation, the constant attention required to confront the auto crisis, along with the ongoing housing problem, will require presidential focus. But there is more. As the recession deepens and the consequent jobs loss continues to expand, President Obama will have to contend with domestic clamor that will certainly force him to spend more time on matters at home, and less attention on events in Afghanistan. How President Obama confronts this issue will be one of many indicators that will determine the future of US policy in Afghanistan.

For many foreign policy analysts President Obama's Afghan strategy indicates that he and his administration will remain engaged in Afghanistan. In Obama's address that unveiled his strategy the president remarked: "I want the American people to understand that we have a clear and focused goal: to disrupt, dismantle, and defeat al Qaeda in Pakistan and Afghanistan, and to prevent their return to either country in the future. That is the goal that must be achieved. That is a cause that could not be more just. And to the terrorists who oppose us, my message is the same: we will defeat you. To achieve our goals, we need a stronger, smarter and comprehensive strategy. To focus on the greatest threat to our people, America must no longer deny resources to Afghanistan because of the war in Iraq. To enhance the military, governance, and economic capacity of Afghanistan and Pakistan, we have to marshal international support. And to defeat an enemy that heeds no borders or laws of war, we must recognize the fundamental connection between the future of Afghanistan and Pakistan—which is why I've appointed Ambassador Richard Holbrooke to serve as Special Representative for both countries, and to work closely with General David Petraeus to integrate our civilian and military efforts."[217]

President Obama made one thing clear: he is now taking ownership of the Afghanistan War. His strategy includes the following critical components:

> I have already ordered the deployment of 17,000 troops that had been requested by General McKiernan for many months. These soldiers and Marines will take the fight to the Taliban in the south and east, and give us a greater capacity to partner with Afghan Security Forces and to go after insurgents along the border. This push will also help provide security in advance of the important presidential election in August. At the same time, we will shift the emphasis of our mission to training and increasing the size of Afghan Security Forces, so that they can eventually take the lead in securing their country. That is how we will prepare Afghans to take responsibility for their security, and how we will ultimately be able to bring our troops home. For three years, our commanders have been clear about the resources they need for training. Those resources have been denied because of the war in Iraq. Now, that will change. The additional troops that we deployed have already increased our training capacity. Later this spring we will deploy approximately 4,000 US troops to train Afghan Security Forces. For the first time, this will fully resource our effort to train and support the Afghan Army and Police. Every American unit in Afghanistan will be partnered with an Afghan unit, and we will seek additional trainers from our NATO allies to ensure that every Afghan unit has a coalition partner. We will accelerate our efforts to build an Afghan Army of 134,000 and a police force of 82,000 so that we can meet these goals by 2011—and increases in Afghan forces may very well be needed as our plans to turn over security responsibility to the Afghans go forward.[218]

An analysis of President Obama's plan reveals a number of important verities. Having examined the strategy many of its components are strikingly similar to President Bush's earlier Iraq War strategies which failed. Second, there is a clear recognition that Afghanistan is now President Obama's war. Third, while the strategy is for the most part sound there are a number of conspicuous weaknesses. To begin with the president is not committed to nation building. What the president and his advisors will learn is that nation building in Afghanistan will be more expensive than may have been realized. No long term sustainable success can occur without a discernable and expansive reconstruction in Afghanistan. Another glaring weakness with the strategy is that President Obama did not reveal or outline an exit strategy. Other problems include the following: what diplomacy is underway to ensure that NATO troops remain at present levels, and similarly, German and Italian troops have performed poorly? It is clear US forces are doing more but what assurances do the American people have that the same level of commitment exists with our NATO partners? Finally, there is another salient dilemma with the strategy: there is no objective to ensure a stable democracy. In fact President Obama's strategy is narrowly tailored: defeat the Taliban and Al Qaeda.

In Pakistan Obama can build on a strategy adjustment made by President Bush. The new strategy called for the increased use of Unmanned Aerial Vehicles (UAVs) to conduct attacks against both al Qaeda and the Taliban in the Federally Administered Tribal Areas (FATA) in Pakistan. Long before the conclusion of President Bush's tenure ample evidence existed to indicate the UAV strikes were successful. Similarly, the offensive strategy has taken the war to the Taliban and al Qaeda; both are now in defensive posture, wondering when and where the next attack will come from. Obama could use this strategy to by time as he conducts his own internal review and develop a hybrid strategy or implement his own approach. If he decides to implement his own strategy there is little doubt it will likely mirror a policy pronouncement made during the campaign: "I will join with our allies in insisting—not simply requesting—that Pakistan crack down on the Taliban, pursue Osama bin Laden and his lieutenants, and end its relationship with all terrorist groups. At the same time, I will encourage dialogue between Pakistan and India to work toward resolving their dispute over Kashmir and between Afghanistan and Pakistan to resolve their historic differences and develop the Pashtun border region. If Pakistan can look toward the east with greater confidence, it will be less likely to believe that its interests are best advanced through cooperation with the Taliban."[219] Obama made a far more comprehensive statement about his intended policy in Pakistan that included the following: "I want to build a broad-based and lasting relationship with the people of Pakistan—not just temporary alliances with their government. While the US and Pakistan must continue to work together to combat terrorism that has claimed innocent lives in both countries and to destroy the terrorist sanctuaries along the Afghan-Pakistani border, I will make helping Pakistan tackle critical challenges like illiteracy, poverty, and lack of health care a key priority including by increasing aid in these areas. I will stand up for democratic institutions, civil society and judicial independence in Pakistan. I cosponsored legislation with Senator Lugar to triple non-military assistance to Pakistan and sustain it for the next decade."[220] These two statements may be the basis of policy, but by themselves they will not resolve the al Qaeda and Taliban safe haven in Pakistan.

During the speech in which Obama revealed his Afghanistan strategy the president made an important point: a stable Pakistan is critical to stability in Afghanistan. On that point Obama's strategy called for confronting the problems within Pakistan and assisting the government with its battle with Pakistani Islamic extremism and confronting al Qaeda and Taliban safe havens. Specifics of his Pakistan strategy include the following:

> Pakistan needs our help in going after al Qaeda. This is no simple task. The tribal regions are vast, rugged, and often ungoverned. That is why we must focus our military assistance on the tools, training and support that Pakistan needs to root out the terrorists. And after years of mixed results, we will not provide a blank check. Pakistan must demonstrate its commitment to rooting out al Qaeda and the violent extremists within its borders. And we will insist that action be taken—one way or another—when we have intelligence about high-level terrorist targets. The government's ability to destroy these safe-havens is tied to its own strength and security. To help Pakistan weather the economic crisis, we must continue to work with the IMF, the World Bank and other international partners. To lessen tensions between two nuclear-armed nations that too often teeter on the edge of escalation and confrontation, we must pursue constructive diplomacy with both India and Pakistan. To avoid the mistakes of the past, we must make clear that our relationship with Pakistan is grounded in support for Pakistan's democratic institutions and the Pakistani people. And to demonstrate through deeds as well as words a commitment that is enduring, we must stand for lasting opportunity. A campaign against extremism will not succeed with bullets or bombs alone. Al Qaeda offers the people of Pakistan nothing but destruction. We stand for something different. So today, I am calling upon Congress to pass a bipartisan bill co-sponsored by John Kerry and Richard Lugar that authorizes $1.5 billion in direct support to the Pakistani people every year over the next five

years—resources that will build schools, roads, and hospitals, and strengthen Pakistan's democracy. I'm also calling on Congress to pass a bipartisan bill co-sponsored by Maria Cantwell, Chris Van Hollen and Peter Hoekstra that creates opportunity zones in the border region to develop the economy and bring hope to places plagued by violence. And we will ask our friends and allies to do their part—including at the donors conference in Tokyo next month. I do not ask for this support lightly. These are challenging times, and resources are stretched. But the American people must understand that this is a down payment on our own future—because the security of our two countries is shared. Pakistan's government must be a stronger partner in destroying these safe-havens, and we must isolate al Qaeda from the Pakistani people. These steps in Pakistan are also indispensable to our effort in Afghanistan, which will see no end to violence if insurgents move freely back and forth across the border. Security demands a new sense of shared responsibility. That is why we will launch a standing, trilateral dialogue among the United States, Afghanistan and Pakistan. Our nations will meet regularly, with Secretary Clinton and Secretary Gates leading our effort. Together, we must enhance intelligence sharing and military cooperation along the border, while addressing issues of common concern like trade, energy, and economic development.[221]

President Obama's new strategy is highly promising. However, there are a host of dilemmas that he will have to overcome. Consistent with Afghanistan, Pakistan is now his issue. Blaming President Bush is no longer an option. Second, President Obama will have to contend with the criticism that if he continues any aspect of President Bush's policy in Pakistan (particularly the billion dollar assistance program, which he has) this decision will undermine his creditability with the left wing of the Democratic Party. Third, because of his electoral mandate and the plethora of other foreign policy issues, Obama will, as did Bush, come to the realization that killing bin Laden will not by itself end the al Qaeda terrorist threat. Finally, there are a number of homegrown threats that are waiting to strike in Europe, and perhaps the United States. If American intelligence failed to detect a terrorist conspiracy, and a major US interest is attacked abroad, what will President Obama do if it is later acknowledged that a Pakistani-based terrorist group is behind the attack?

During the transition period then President-elect Obama received a lesson in the always tempestuous process of crisis management. The terrorist attack in Mumbai, India offered Obama access to President Bush's national security team and the personal diplomacy that he and Secretary of State Condoleezza Rice employed to avert a subsequent crisis between India and Pakistan. The administrations diplomatic efforts marked the second time that a terrorist attack had been used to spark conflict between India and Pakistan. Previously, in the wake of the terrorist attack that killed members of India's parliament in late 2001, an Indo-Pak war had been prevented when Secretary of State Colin Powell and his deputy Richard Armitage forestalled conflict between two nuclear states. One will hope that Obama will learn from the crises and understand the necessity of direct involvement of the United States to prevent a war among coalition partners in the war on terror. Second, there is another issue that Obama should comprehend: the crisis appeared to be an attempt to undermine what terrorists construed was his impending strategy. On this point consider the words of Pratap Bhanu Mehta, the head of the Centre for Policy Research, who made this statement: "This attack was not just an attempt to scuttle India's peace process with Pakistan. It was in many ways a pre-emptive strike against [Barack] Obama's strategy for the region."[222]

As the Obama administration concludes its internal policy review in the Indian Sub-Continent, the president and his senior advisors will have to understand that al Qaeda and its affiliates in the region—to include the Pakistani terrorist group Lashkar-e-Taiba, for example—will work to disrupt the administrations strategy which will be aimed at reducing the influence of bin Laden's transnational empire. Similarly, Obama will have to stay engaged to ensure that the terrorist objective (fomenting unrest or inducing a war between India and Pakistan, either of which will increase recruitment of al Qaeda or its affiliates) never materializes. If Obama fails in this regard the war on terror could move to a dangerous level with the terrorists obtaining momentum and expanding safe havens in the region.

The war on terror offers additional opportunities and dilemmas that involve strategy. For starters during the presidential campaign Obama made a significant statement about his intentions to move beyond President Bush's approach to confronting transnational terrorism: "We must forge a more effective global response to the terrorism that came to our shores on an unprecedented scale on 9/11."[223] Before addressing this statement it is important to note that many within Obama's own party did not like the fact that on the one hand he made a declaration to end the war in Iraq but they were surprised and dismayed that he was expanding another war. Nancy Pelosi, the Speaker of the House, is perhaps one of the most important individuals to express opposition to expanding the war in Afghanistan. As one would surmise there other critics.

> Unfortunately, Obama has given some mixed messages about whether he is going to end the "war on terror" and the wrongheaded policies that have resulted from it. His most troubling statements concern Afghanistan and Osama bin Laden. In his debates with McCain, Obama consistently charged that the US had "taken its eye off the ball" in Afghanistan and had failed to make capturing or killing bin Laden its top priority. These arguments, while not untrue, implicitly legitimize the "war on terror," and simply critique Bush for fighting it in the wrong way. Obama's proposal to escalate the US war in Afghanistan, though qualified by his greater emphasis on rebuilding the country, seems to indicate that he believes the Taliban can be defeated militarily. This is a recipe for failure: As former British Foreign Service officer Rory Stewart noted in the *New York Times*, the US military buildup in Afghanistan has inflamed the Taliban resistance and made the situation worse. In a recent interview on "60 Minutes," Obama said he would make capturing or killing bin Laden a top priority, and he has threatened to strike terrorist targets inside Pakistan if the Pakistan government proved unwilling or unable to do so.[224]

Gary Kamiya, the individual that authored the above statement, made this additional comment: "But it is just as important that Obama immediately declare an end to the "war on terror," and reverse all of the policies that have been carried out in its name."[225]

The opinion expressed above is emblematic of the position taken by many in the Democratic Party, and among those outside the party. At issue, is the position to end the war on terror realistic, particularly when there is salient evidence that al Qaeda has reconstituted itself, and there is concern that a major attack is on the horizon? Many would argue that such a position is representative of a trend that indicates that support for the war on terror is waning. A Pew Research poll taken in 2006 indicates that international support for the war is declining: "Nearly five years after the September 11, 2001 attacks, international support for the US-led war on terrorism continues to wane. Outside of the US only two countries—India and Russia—register majority support for the war on terror, and it remains particularly unpopular in predominantly Muslim countries, although support has risen eight points since last year among Pakistani's, whose government is a key partner in efforts to combat Al Qaeda. Among several of America's traditional allies, support has fallen steeply since 2002, and it has virtually collapsed in two countries, Spain and Japan. In the former, the percentage of those who favor US efforts against terrorism now stands at 19%, down from 63% in 2003, while among Japanese it has tumbled from 61% in 2002 to 26% today."[226]

Thus it is not unusual to read statements urging Obama to end the war on terror. There is little doubt however that Obama will ignore the calls for ending the war on terror; he recognizes the decline in support for the war on terror is principally a function of the global view the Iraq war increased not just anti-Americanism, but Operation Iraq Freedom caused the loss of America's moral authority to conduct the war on terror. An increase in moral authority can return if President Obama successfully prosecutes the war elsewhere. Similarly, one of the great failures of President Bush's prosecution of the war on terror is that in the wake of the public relations disaster following the commencement of the Iraq War, the war on terror, from a global perspective, was always viewed through the prism of events in that country. The incessant statement that Iraq "is the central front" in the war on terror further undercut the Bush administration's effort to sustain domestic and global support for the war.

To reverse this trend President Obama will have to regain American and international attention about the significance of the war. If Obama is serious about "a more effective global response to terrorism" he is in many ways the perfect American president to launch a "rhetorical blitz" to refocus attention on the war on terror. Indeed, he promised to introduce a program to address the dilemmas associated with public diplomacy:

> I will also launch a program of public diplomacy that is a coordinated effort across my Administration, not a small group of political officials at the State Department explaining a misguided war. We will open "America Houses" in cities across the Islamic world, with Internet, libraries, English lessons, stories of America's Muslims and the strength they add to our country, and vocational programs. Through a new "America's Voice Corps" we will recruit, train, and send out into the field talented young Americans who can speak with—and listen to—the people who today hear about us only from our enemies.[227]

President Obama is blessed with oratory skills that rival those of President Ronald Reagan, the "great communicator." However, President Obama will have to confront a political reality: with the economy continuing to spiral downward, he will have to manage time carefully in terms of his foreign policy pronouncements. That is with the unemployment rate unlikely to decline anytime soon President Obama will have a domestic population clamoring for answers about reversing the economic recession and therefore it follows the American population will be less concerned about foreign policy. Second, will Obama keep another pledge? Obama noted in an address at the Wilson Center in Washington, D.C., on August 1, 2007, that "As President, I will lead this effort. In the first 100 days of my Administration, I will travel to a major Islamic forum [that place is Turkey, April 2009] and deliver an address to redefine our struggle. I will make clear that we are not at war with Islam, that we will stand with those who are willing to stand up for their future, and that we need their effort to defeat the prophets of hate and violence. I will speak directly to that child who looks up at that helicopter, and my message will be clear: 'You matter to us. Your future is our future. And our moment is now.'"[228] President Obama met this pledge during his trip to Cairo, Egypt on June 4, 2009.

President Obama's effort to convince the Islamic world that the US-led war is not aimed at all Muslims is indeed appropriate. That said the president attempt redefine what the US calls the war on terror is problematic and a waste of time. President Obama and elements within the foreign policy establishment have settled on the phrase "Overseas Contingency Operation" or OCO to replace the "Global War on Terror" or GWOT. This is not the first time the US government has attempted to move away from the global war on terror verbiage. During the Bush administration Secretary of Defense Donald Rumsfeld came up with Global Struggle Against Violent Extremism or GSAVE. President Bush quickly dismissed the idea and the GWOT remained the acronym. Now we are entering a new period in which the current administration is attempting to place its stamp on the war on terror. There is little doubt the change is alarming and reversing a trend in which the US government had a clear sense of direction for the most expansive war of the twenty first century. Critics charge the term "Overseas Contingency Operation" smacks of a pre-9/11 mindset, one that reduces forces on the war in an effort to confront a burgeoning set of domestic challenges.

There is little doubt that Bush's post-9/11 strategy will remain as the fundamental strategy of President Obama. When Obama used the words "forge a more effective global response" against international terrorism, the perception herein is that this does not mean that President Obama will alter much of the essential components of President Bush's strategy against terror.[229] What Obama will likely do is end American support for or in involvement with torture. Second, he will likely do away with the Bush Doctrine and aspects of the policy of preemption. Taking these two steps will be critical in Obama's efforts to restore the image of the United States abroad. But these are the easy steps for President Obama.

With regard to the difficult aspects of providing a more effective strategy, President Obama will have to address the following critical questions, all of which will determine just how effective he will be in conducting the war on terror. The questions include the following: What adjustments will President Obama make in conducting the war on terror? How will Obama confront al Qaeda? Will President Obama fight the war in clearly defined phases, or will he conduct the war on terror on an ad hoc basis?

Well into his administration Obama has not indicated that he is willing to make a sharp departure from his predecessors' strategy. Much of this is a function of the prioritization of the economy, but there is another reason: "if it isn't broken don't fix it." Thus the center of gravity—the four pronged strategy—will continue. There is little doubt, if the internal review is apolitical, that President Obama is unlikely to make any changes in this area. That said there will be changes elsewhere. To understand this point it is essential to recall a major statement made by Obama during the presidential campaign. On August 1, 2007 Obama made the following statement about the need for a comprehensive strategy:

> We did not finish the job against al Qaeda in Afghanistan. We did not develop new capabilities to defeat a new enemy, or launch a comprehensive strategy to dry up the

terrorists' base of support.... Al Qaeda terrorists train, travel, and maintain global communications in this safe-haven. The Taliban pursues a hit and run strategy, striking in Afghanistan, [and] then skulking across the border to safety. This is the wild frontier of our globalized world. There are wind-swept deserts and cave-dotted mountains. There are tribes that see borders as nothing more than lines on a map, and governments as forces that come and go. There are blood ties deeper than alliances of convenience, and pockets of extremism that follow religion to violence. It's a tough place. But that is no excuse. There must be no safe haven for terrorists who threaten America. We cannot fail to act because action is hard. As President, I would make hundreds of millions of dollars in US military aid to Pakistan conditional, and I would make our conditions clear: Pakistan must make substantial progress in closing down the training camps, evicting foreign fighters, and preventing the Taliban from using Pakistan as a staging area for attacks in Afghanistan. It is time to turn the page. It is time to write a new chapter in our response to 9/11.[230]

This excerpt is replete with significant statements. That is the initial point. With regard to the second point it is essential to note that Barack Obama never made a more significant statement on the issue of strategy and the war on terror. That said the statement on strategy is problematic on a number of fronts. Obama talks about "a comprehensive strategy to dry up terrorist base of support." Obama is correct on this point. The issue is that he does not provide any specifics as to how he would resolve the problem.

Second, defining the threat posed by a safe haven represents the first of many dilemmas that confronts Obama. Here are just a few of the issues that Obama will have to contend with. He will have to prioritize when and where he strikes. Additionally, in defining when and where he strikes, Obama will have to comprehend, through consultation with the Pentagon and the State Department, the politico-military consequences of expanding the war on terror into the next phase. Third, domestically Obama will have to make the case for the next phase. This is critical because given that fixing the economy is his central mandate, too much focus on "then next war" could be politically damaging. Fourth, there is the converse argument: the wars in Afghanistan, Iraq and dealing with al Qaeda remain threats to US security and therefore they can not be dismissed simply because of America's economic woes. In effect President Obama will have to select (or perhaps use both) between two foreign policy schools. The Jeffersonian school calls for dealing with domestic issues (safe guarding democracy at home, and in this context, dealing with the economy, healthcare, education etc.,) and avoiding international issues, particularly wars because they increase national debt, and that debt will impact future generations. These are some of the basic tenets of Jeffersonian school. Then there is the Jacksonian school which observes that when the country is attacked there "is no substitute for victory." In short the security of the country is the singular focus of the president during war time. Thus the economy is considered by many, under these circumstances, to be secondary. Barack Obama, consistent with President Franklin Delano Roosevelt, introduced his version of the "new deal," with the desire of trying to rapidly decrease the pain of the "great recession." In this regard he is betting that fixing the ailing economy, his mandate, is more essential than the security of the country.

Finally there are two additional dilemmas. The list of al Qaeda safe havens is a long one. Some of the major locations around the globe include Pakistan, Somalia, Indonesia, Iraq, Yemen, within the Palestinian refugee camps in Lebanon, to name a few. Obama will be unable to contend military with the host of safe havens around the world. The US military is too overstretched and he will need major coalition support to contend with the voluminous safe havens for al Qaeda and its affiliates around the world. Then there is the cost factor; it could cost the treasury tens of billions of dollars to deal effectively with the safe havens that are used by al Qaeda. Given the global financial crisis the United States can not count on major support from its allies around the world. Second, Obama talked about linking US military assistance to Pakistan's success in closing down training camps and safe havens inside the country. There is evidence to support Obama's position. As a Pentagon report noted in Pakistan "Al Qaeda and other violent extremists continue to hide out in the FATA, where they are able to recruit, train, and target US and western interests, including plots against Europe and the US homeland.... Despite successful attacks against some terrorist <u>training</u> facilities in the tribal areas, it is believed other camps remain active and safe havens have grown in recent years.... It may be several years before Pakistan's comprehensive strategy to render the remote tribal areas permanently inhospitable to terrorists, insurgents and other violent extremists can be measured for success."[231] The problem is that linkage in this form would be a political and diplomatic disaster. President Obama should be mindful that Pakistan has lost hundreds of troops in its efforts to contend with the Al Qaeda/Taliban threat in FATA. At another level, any linkage connecting US assistance to Pakistani performance will be used by Islamist forces to undermine the US-Pakistani relationship, which if it were to occur, could lead to a loss of a major ally in the war on terror and cede to al Qaeda a permanent base.

These issues notwithstanding, President Obama, with respect to the war on terror, should set realistic objectives. One of President Bush's major mistakes involves the use of rhetoric that calls for "the defeat of terrorism in our lifetime." No country or series of states will ever defeat terrorism in its entirety. Instead, collective actions by states may defeat al Qaeda and contain the scourge of terrorism. Similarly, Obama should end the talk that he will get Osama bin Laden. In a *CBS* "60 Minutes" interview Obama strongly asserted that "It is a top priority for us to stamp out Al Qaeda once and for all" and that "capturing or killing Bin Laden is a critical aspect of stamping out Al Qaeda." There is little doubt that "stamping out al Qaeda" is a welcomed objective but without a discernable strategy for doing it the statement amounts to empty rhetoric. On killing bin Laden, and making it a priority, the obvious question is this: what if he fails? President Obama should understand the dilemmas posed by prioritizing killing bin Laden. First, President Bush used the slogan "wanted dead or alive" when boasting about his objective to kill bin Laden. In the end Bush failed to kill bin Laden, and this is now a component of his presidential legacy. Now Obama has once again made killing bin Laden a priority; the failure to do so, as it did with Bush, will comprise an aspect of Obama's legacy. Second, there is another dilemma in prioritizing the killing of bin Laden: are you willing to mount a military assault to complete the objective and deal with the attendant consequences. Assuming that bin Laden is in the FATA region rest assured there is large force protecting him, and they would die to protect him. Therefore, President Obama will have to comprehend that capturing or killing bin Laden involves political risks. Third, there is this reality: killing bin Laden will not by itself end the transnational empire. The network will survive long after the death of bin Laden.

There are a number of additional opportunities for President Obama. But as we will see, the opportunities, if Obama fails to seize the moment, could quickly shift to a nightmare for Obama should he not demonstrate leadership. In both Afghanistan and in Iraq President Bush succeeded in completing the initial military objective: regime change; both the Taliban and Saddam Hussein were deposed. That said President Bush failed miserably in postwar reconstruction (stability operations in military parlance). The opportunity for President Obama is a fundamental one: If he succeeds in Afghanistan and Iraq, completing the postwar phases, he has the opportunity to be on hand for a signature moment in American history, a reference to the certain victory parades for returning US troops down the "canyon of heroes: or down the "great white way" in Times Square in New York City. However, if he fails to successfully conclude each war there are dilemmas that may negatively impact his legacy. For example, Afghanistan could possibly turn into a disaster. Consider this possible scenario. Having campaigned for increase in US troops to defeat the Taliban, what would happen if the US death toll increased as a result of this policy shift? With the specter of increasing US troop deaths in Afghanistan (the reader should note that in Iraq in the opening months of the surge American troop deaths increased dramatically) will President Obama have the stomach to see the strategy adjustments through to the end, or will he succumb to "casualty phobia" as American's, fed up with the loses, begin to protest US involvement and begin to request an immediate withdrawal of American military forces? This scenario is interesting in that it places Obama in the similar situation of his predecessor President Bush. Remember it was President Bush in an ever-expanding insurgency that refused to consider withdrawal. If Obama does confront the reality of a dramatic increase in US casualties in Afghanistan, is he willing to confront the near certain criticism from Republican's that he destroyed the opportunity presented by Bush, and that on his watch the situation in Afghanistan is now worse?

As terrorist experts examine President Obama's strategy several indicators will be front and center. First, to what extent, if any, is Obama's strategy consistent with or an alteration of Bush's fundamental four pronged strategy? If Obama undertakes a major transformation in this area, he will be measured by the extent to which he prevented an attack on the homeland, or and attack against US far-flung interests abroad. Second, the focus of Obama's strategy is itself significant. Throughout the presidential campaign Obama made it clear that Afghanistan and Pakistan are the central nodes of his strategy. Additionally, Obama in repeated statements in the campaign made it clear that Afghanistan, not Iraq is the central front on the war on terror. In many ways the president is correct, however, losing Pakistan to al Qaeda and the Taliban will have far greater consequences for the US-led war on terrorism. Obama, as mentioned earlier, will increase US troops in Afghanistan, again a process that was long underway under Bush, but a critical question, and one that should be debated in the Congress, is whether or not Obama will expand upon Bush's strategy to deploy unmanned drones and other assets to target al Qaeda and the Taliban in the FATA within the lawless regions of Pakistan? The answer to this question will indicate the seriousness of purpose for Obama and the war on terror.

Third, there is little doubt that al Qaeda or its affiliates is planning an attack against the homeland or they are planning to target US interests around the world. How President Obama responds to this scenario will provide a barometer on his leadership proclivities. If for example he adopts the policy that "terrorism should be treated as a law enforcement issue" such a response could prove disastrous, and American's can anticipate an increase in attacks against the US interests. Should he provide a measured response where the president identifies the threat and launches a clearly defined politico-military response, he will be praised in much the way President Bush was during the mid-September-December 2001 period. Rest assured his response, and the subsequent strategy that flows from such an attack, will represent initial indicators of President Obama's leadership of the war on terror.

Fourth, for many experts President Obama's stunning silence on other critical components of the war on terror has not engendered support, but rather concern. For example, President Bush's supplemental strategy in Africa has proven successful in preventing al Qaeda or its allies from establishing safe havens or bases in the region. It remains unknown the extent to which President Obama will continue or scale back this strategy. If and when the president commences an internal debate with his senior advisors on this issue, he should take into account that many states that are members of the coalition fear that the United States, once its interests have been achieved, will abandon them. The lesson of Pakistan is instructive. Once the Soviets withdrew from Afghanistan, the US shut down the "outpost" in Pakistan, and did nothing to contain or assist our ally with the virulent Islamic radicalism that came to dominate that country. Today we are still paying for that decision. Thus it is critical that Obama not repeat this mistake in Africa or with other allies scattered around the world.

Fifth, the issue of "presidential focus" will be another critical measure in assessing Obama's stewardship of the war on terror. Given that the economy represents his mandate, and that many analysts anticipate a long recession, it is not a stretch to observe that President Obama could be overwhelmed by events at home and this could decrease his attention to the war on terror. It is this scenario that greatly concerns military commanders and those in the scholarly community. Will President Obama strike a balance between domestic and foreign policy issues, particularly the war on terror? Conversely, there is another issue: will the war on terror overwhelm the president's economic mandate? Each proposition is troubling for Obama. Striking a balance would represent the best of all worlds for President Obama. But given the country is at war on multiple fronts, there are those that will argue attention to America's security outweighs the economy. That said Obama, consistent with Clinton, argued the strength of the economy is a barometer or measure of US power. This view is perhaps a window into how President Obama may proceed. Should the war on terror eclipse President Obama's economic mandate, particularly if the economy continues to spiral downward, this could undermine his electoral coalition and prevent his reelection. And if he mishandles the war on terror, then this could lead to an enduring negative legacy.

CONCLUSION

"It's the economy, stupid." Back in the 1992 campaign, that one line told us that Bill Clinton did not intend to be a great foreign policy president."[232] Stephen Walt is the author of this sobering assessment of the Clinton years' in US foreign policy. A question begs, given the state of the American economy, is this statement suggestive of a pending reality for President Obama's stewardship of US foreign policy?

The point is not to suggest that the economy is not essential. There is little doubt that not only is the economy President Obama's mandate, but it is by far the issue that will occupy the opening year-plus of his presidency. Rather, the point herein is to state that the lack of attention to foreign policy can undermine a presidency and lead to untold problems. Richard Haass, currently the president of the Council on Foreign Relations validates the aforementioned point by making this telling statement.

> Despite some noteworthy achievements in foreign as well as domestic policy, the Clinton era was marked by a preference for symbolism over substance and short-term crisis management over long-term strategizing. Unlike domestic policy, however, foreign policy suffered from a lack of presidential interest, attention, and respect. It suffered, in short, from malign neglect.[233]

Does this statement portend the future legacy of President Obama? Perhaps, but one may conclude that it is way too early for such an assessment. Indeed, some will argue that far more evidence is required. They would be correct. That being the case, Haass' comments represent a caveat of a pending reality if President Obama ignores the ever-growing foreign policy problems that will impact his administration. As the final section demonstrates the Democratic dilemma may be President Obama's most telling problem.

OVERCOMING THE DEMOCRATIC FOREIGN POLICY DILEMMA

The Democratic foreign policy dilemma is by no means new. Indeed it is historic. The point in this conclusion is to demonstrate how four dilemmas have significantly affected the governance of Democratic stewardship of US foreign policy after they succeeded Republican presidential administrations. The first dilemma is acute and significantly impacted last the two Democratic Presidents, President Jimmy Carter and President Bill Clinton. The dilemma in question is that Democratic Presidents have boasted of the reorientation of US foreign policy and restoring the image of America. Second, each of the aforementioned Democratic Presidents had to confront "the politics of exile." Third, in coming to power after the conclusion of Republican administrations, a host of foreign policy fiascoes frustrated both Carter and Clinton. Fourth, the Democratic stewardship of US foreign policy had this added dimension: the bulk of the issues they confronted were bequeathed to them by Republican Presidents. Finally, viewed collectively, these dilemmas, as described in detail below, will impact President Obama in ways that are far worse then his Democratic predecessors. The problems that are likely to develop for President Obama are possibly so damaging as to produce a foreign policy recognized for a legacy less of productive change, and more for failing to adequately deal with a plethora of foreign policy issues.

The commonalities of Carter and Clinton are that each endeavored to reorient US foreign policy and restore America's image abroad. Both met with failure. For Carter Human Rights occupied the center of gravity. The human rights driven foreign policy agenda had been designed to supplant the Nixon-Kissinger policy of détente. That said Carter's human rights policy was an unmitigated disaster. The policy suffered in part because President Carter far too often targeted US allies and too little attention was given to the humans rights abuses of communist countries.

President Clinton had a difficult challenge. With the Cold War over, Clinton had the unenviable difficult task of finding a replacement for containment. Having launched "enlargement and engagement," the strategy immediately met with criticism. In do course Clinton's strategy of enlargement and engagement slipped from the headlines.

Second, Carter and Clinton both had to confront what David Broader referred to as the "politics of exile." In this political environment a number of problems impacted the foreign policy leadership of both Democratic Presidents. The issue that Carter and Clinton confronted, having been on the political sidelines for an extended period, is that they were forced to play catch up to world events, and then implement "a clear and workable foreign policy vision." After eight years of Republican dominance (Richard M. Nixon, 1969-1974 and Gerald R. Ford, 1974-1977) of the White House Carter emerged from exile as the US president forced to conduct foreign policy in the shadows of the Vietnam War. Additionally, three issues affected President Carter's stewardship of US foreign policy: the need for a post-Détente policy, the requirement to restore the battered American image in the wake of the defeat in Vietnam, and third, the president needed to restore public confidence in the wake of the Watergate scandal. During a one term presidency Carter failed to overcome the politics of exile. As evidence of his failure, the Iran hostage crisis (and the attendant failed rescue attempt) is perhaps his most enduring foreign policy legacy.

In the case of President Clinton he came to power after twelve years of Republican rule (Ronald W. Reagan, 1981-1989 and George H. W. Bush, 1989-1993). By the time he entered office he had a series of issues to confront. Like Carter he had to contend with the reality that there would be no continuity between his administrations policies and those of his predecessors. Clinton's singular predicament is that with the Cold War over he had the untenable responsibility of devising a strategic replacement for containment, but it was by no means the only one. In the post-cold war era there were new challenges and threats. Those threats ranged from terrorism, ethnic-conflicts, nuclear proliferation, and genocide (Rwanda and in Bosnia), to name a few. With respect to these issues Clinton had to confront the reality that each could and at times did eclipse his economic mandate.

A third similarity is that foreign policy fiascoes frustrated both Carter and Clinton. The Iran hostage crisis, the failure to prevent the Soviet invasion of Afghanistan, and the Sandinista takeover over in Nicaragua, are salient examples of the debacles that occurred during Carter's tenure. For Clinton the list of foreign policy fiascoes were equally problematic. Clinton's failures include Somalia, Haiti, and Bosnia, all of which occurred during his first year in office. In the second year the president's mishandling of the genocide in Rwanda represented another major foreign policy fiasco. But sadly there were others. The most significant of which involved the failure to confront terrorism. In this respect the bombing of the World Trade Center in 1993, the destruction of US embassies in Kenya and Tanzania in 1998, and the bombing of USS Cole in 2000 indicate the pervasive nature of the Al Qaeda transnational terror network, and the absence of a credible American response.

Fourth, Carter and Clinton were both bequeathed "unfinished foreign policy issues" (also referred to as the "inherited phenomenon") from Republican presidents that impacted their administrations. In the case of Carter he had to deal with a host of left over problems from the Nixon-Ford years. Those issues include dealing with the Soviet Union, the continuation of diplomacy with China; Middle East peace negotiations, dealing with the chaos in Cambodia, confronting Ford's failed policies across Africa (particularly in Apartheid South Africa, Rhodesia, and Zaire), and dealing with the repressive dictatorships in Latin America, represented some of the foreign policy challenges that awaited President Carter.

With regard to Clinton the list was far more expansive. George H.W. Bush bequeathed the following issues to President Clinton: Iraq, Iran, North Korea, Haiti, Somalia, Bosnia, the future of NATO, Middle East Peace, the post-Cold War future of US military strategy, confronting bilateral relationship challenges with Russia, China, and Japan, ethnic conflicts in Central Europe, Africa and Asia (East Timor), confronting the threat of nuclear proliferation, and NAFTA represented the plethora of foreign policy issues that awaited President Clinton. These issues are far more problematic when one takes into account that Clinton had an electoral mandate to fix the economy.

Taken collectively the records of Carter and Clinton in confronting the Democratic foreign policy dilemma is one of failure. Equally important in considering the impact of the failures of the two previous Democratic presidents during their efforts to confront the "dilemma" is the recognition of several significant realities. The first is that the "dilemma" does not mean that Carter and Clinton did not have foreign policy successes. To the contrary they both had successes. In the case of President Carter some of his accomplishments include the Camp David Peace Accord, The Panama Canal Treaty, and the Recognition of China. In the case of President Clinton he had a number of accomplishments that include the successful negotiation of the Comprehensive Test Ban Treaty, the Good Friday Agreement, participation in the Rome Treaty and the Kyoto Protocol. In the end the impact of the dilemma for the Democrat Party is two fold: the efforts to shift US foreign policy not only met with failure but in the case of both Carter and Clinton a host of foreign policy fiascoes littered the landscape impacting the American image and producing negative foreign policy legacies.

The second reality is that in response to the decline of the American image under Carter and Clinton and the perception that both lack resolve with regard to the use of force, a dramatic pendulum swing occurs during Republican presidents once they supplant Democratic presidents (Carter and Clinton). First Republican presidents are more apt to reassert American primacy and in the case of Bush several important shifts occurred: the decline of multilateralism (the increase in the unilateralism) and the increase in the use of force (preemptive and preventive). These shifts during the Bush administration are critical to understanding the Democratic foreign policy dilemma and its impact on President Barack Obama.

In the contemporary presidency of Barack Obama the aforementioned dilemmas are far worse, and any of which taken individually, in multiple combinations or collectively could overwhelm his economic mandate, and could lead to one of the worst foreign policy legacies in history.

There is little doubt that the severe financial crisis is the "urgent priority" of Obama's presidency. That said while there is little doubt that the economic crisis is not a problem created by President Obama, he is in a far worse situation then his Democratic predecessors. Carter had to deal with stagflation which is an economic situation in which inflation (double-digit inflation occurred under Carter) and economic stagnation occurred concurrently. Clinton had to deal with a recession and ballooning budget deficits that emerged out of the Reagan-Bush years. In the words of economist Nouriel Roubini Obama confronts a major challenge: "The most severe recession in 50 years; the worst financial and banking crisis since the Great Depression; a ballooning fiscal deficit that may be as high as a trillion dollars in 2009 and 2010."[234] That said both Carter and Clinton discovered foreign policy issues have a life of their own, and they can and will overwhelm (on occasion) a president's domestic agenda. There is little doubt that a similar reality awaits President Obama. At issue, why is this reality a near certainty?

To address this question it is important return to the four Democratic dilemmas outlined above. Carter and Clinton upon entering office moved quickly to shift away from Republican policies. In both cases such attempts were not only understandable but anticipated. It was the outcome that proved unfortunate: both failed in their efforts to alter the course of US foreign policy and failed to restore America's image. Even more troubling for the Democratic Party in subsequent presidential elections (after Carter, Reagan assumes office; and after Clinton, George W. Bush became president; significantly both Republican presidents served two terms) the incoming Republican presidents wasted little time in discarding the policies of Carter and then Clinton.

In the case of President Obama he entered office determined to transform US foreign policy. He incessantly spoke of doing away with President Bush's politics of fear, and replacing them with the politics of hope. During the presidential campaign Senator Obama offered this statement to underscore his desire to redirect US foreign policy:

Today we are again called to provide visionary leadership. This century's threats are at least as dangerous and in some ways more complex than those we have confronted in the past. They come from weapons that can kill on a mass scale and from global terrorists who respond to alienation or perceived injustice with murderous nihilism. They come from rogue states allied to terrorists and from rising powers that could challenge both America and the international foundation of liberal democracy. They come from weak states that cannot control their territory or provide for their people. And they come from a warming planet that will spur new diseases, spawn more devastating natural disasters, and catalyze deadly conflicts. To recognize the number and complexity of these threats is not to give way to pessimism. Rather, it is a call to action. These threats demand a new vision of leadership in the twenty-first century—a vision that draws from the past but is not bound by outdated thinking. The Bush administration responded to the unconventional attacks of 9/11 with conventional thinking of the past, largely viewing problems as state-based and principally amenable to military solutions. It was this tragically misguided view that led us into a war in Iraq that never should have been authorized and never should have been waged. In the wake of Iraq and Abu Ghraib, the world has lost trust in our purposes and our principles. After thousands of lives lost and billions of dollars spent, many Americans may be tempted to turn inward and cede our leadership in world affairs. But this is a mistake we must not make. America cannot meet the threats of this century alone, and the world cannot meet them without America. We can neither retreat from the world nor try to bully it into submission. We must lead the world, by deed and by example. Such leadership demands that we retrieve a fundamental insight of Roosevelt, Truman, and Kennedy—one that is truer now than ever before: the security and well-being of each and every American depend on the security and well-being of those who live beyond our borders. The mission of the United States is to provide global leadership grounded in the understanding that the world shares a common security and a common humanity. The American moment is not over, but it must be seized anew. To see American power in terminal decline is to ignore America's great promise and historic purpose in the world. If elected president, I will start renewing that promise and purpose the day I take office.[235]

During the opening months of his presidency Obama's central focus remains the economy. The soaring campaign rhetoric that called for the renewal of American leadership, for now, is none existent. Secretary of State Hillary Clinton, given the opportunity to fill this void, has said and done nothing of consequence. The Obama administration, as expected, discarded the Bush Doctrine, but an Obama Doctrine, at the time of this writing, is still unfolding, and thus it is too early to make an assessment of its success or failure.

The burgeoning economic crisis, dubbed by some as the "great recession," will make the "politics of exile" far more arduous for President Obama. Though Obama's administration is replete with officials that have tremendous foreign policy experience, there are two reasons why experience will not develop as a factor to militate against exile politics. First, many of these same officials came to their positions of influence at a time when Clinton had to confront the challenges posed by the politics of exile. This group of foreign policy advisors failed to confront a host of issues that emerged in the post-Cold War era. Now in the post-September World it is highly unlikely that they will successfully manage the wars in Iraq and Afghanistan and then resurrect the global war on terrorism. Second, as an attendant issue, those same experienced individuals scattered across the foreign policy bureaucracy are led by two inexperienced individuals: Obama and Clinton. President Obama's inexperience is well documented and there is no need to restate what is already known. In the case of Secretary of State Clinton, she lacks the intellectual prowess (this is a problem that transcends Clinton, and is found in the previous leaders of the state department) and a vision to defeat the ghosts of exile.

The third dilemma is equally troubling for President Obama. As noted above, Carter and Clinton were bequeathed "unfinished foreign policy issues" from Republican presidents that impacted their administrations. In the case of Obama unfortunately President Bush's "unfinished" foreign policy issues are far more expansive than anything experienced by the two previous Democratic Presidents.[236] The list of left over foreign policy problems include the following: two wars, Iraq and Afghanistan, managing the global war on terror, preventing a terrorist attack on the homeland, Pakistan, the regional threat posed by Iran, the continuing problem of nuclear proliferation in North Korea, Middle East Peace (made more difficult in wake of the Hamas-Israeli conflict in Gaza), dealing with the rise of Russia and China, the global financial crisis, National Missile Defense System, Global Warming, restoring the American image, finding a guiding foreign policy framework that will finally supplant containment, ending torture and rendition, finding a home for the 250 high valued terrorists that are housed in the detention facility in Guantánamo Bay, Cuba, shutting down the "black prisons" scattered around the world, Narco-Terrorism in Mexico, dealing with the Somalia (not just the piracy, but a far more significant set of issues await Obama to include: the al Qaeda safe haven that exists in Somalia and the rise of radical Islam), genocide in Darfur, Sudan, restoring Indo-Pak relations in the wake of the terrorist attack in Mumbai, India, are some, but not all of the issues that have been bequeathed to him by President Bush.

One of the frightening responsibilities, indeed challenges, confronting Obama is how to prioritize them. It is for his advisors, and for the president to conclude whether Iraq or Afghanistan, or keeping the American people safe from a future terrorist strike against a major terrorist attack will be the foreign policy issues that will dominate his administration. But there are other factors that will dictate which foreign policy issues will become the focus of his administration. The challenge of fixing the ailing economy will remain at the top of the presidential agenda. As we have already witnessed President Obama expended significant political capital managing the great recession. The more time dealing with the economy translates into decreased presidential focus on foreign policy. Second, prioritization may have little to do with the White House calculus, but may be determined by evolving crises abroad. These crises will be a pivotal factor in determining what issues dominate the foreign policy agenda of President Obama. Third, both Carter and Clinton adopted an ad hoc approach in confronting the Democratic dilemma. In the case of President Clinton this proved particularly alarming because his economic strategy had not taken hold and he haphazardly turned to foreign policy in order to escape domestic clamor. As this excerpt demonstrates the results of the precipitous shift to foreign policy proved disastrous:

> President Clinton's foreign policy, rather than protecting American national interests, has pursued social work worldwide. Three failed interventions in 1993—in Bosnia, in Somalia, and the first try in Haiti—illustrate this dramatically. Preoccupied with "helping the helpless," the administration alienated vital allies, changed direction repeatedly to repair Clinton's sagging image.[237]

This haphazard prioritization of foreign policy impacted Clinton's image at home and abroad. This history is important for President Obama in one significant way: this is course that he should not select. In the end dealing with the inherited phenomenon is and will be a major challenge for President Obama during his stewardship of US foreign policy.

The fourth dilemma (foreign policy fiascoes) represents a critical measure, but at present it can not used to define the Obama administration. That is no foreign policy fiasco has yet occurred. There are reasons to assert that one or more will. Historically speaking all post-World War II presidents, Democrats and Republicans, have unfortunately been involved in foreign policy fiascoes. A few examples exemplify the point. For Nixon the Salvador Allende Affair and the secret bombings in Cambodia demonstrate his capacity of foreign policy mismanagement; for Reagan the Iran-Contra Affair is perhaps his most salient foreign policy misadventure. For Clinton the firefight in Mogadishu, Somalia, in October of 1993, along with Operation Infinite Reach are other examples of his foreign policy fiascoes, and finally, the Iraq War represents a foreign policy misadventure for President George W. Bush. Thus while it is the case that no misadventure has occurred history dictates that in time one will develop during the Obama administration.

There may indeed be a fifth factor: expectation. During the tenures of Carter and Clinton both envisage the dilemmas of rising expectations. After the Nixon-Ford and Reagan-George H.W. Bush years, Democrats clamored for a departure from the policies they believed not only damaged the American image abroad but also the fact that Republican presidents routinely betrayed traditional foreign policy values. Therefore when Carter and later Clinton entered office the expectations for the restoration of the American image and a return to traditional foreign policy values were high on the agenda for both presidents. Both presidents made tremendous strides in both areas but ultimately they failed. Within the Democratic foreign policy establishment there were open expressions of disappointment, not only because of the failed attempts, but that such failures were used by Republican presidential candidates (Reagan and George W. Bush) as a vehicle to retake the White House. For President Obama the expectations among Democrats in the United States (and the equally important expectations of change around the world) for dramatic changes in foreign policy is far more pronounced than during the periods when Carter and Clinton entered the White House. With the inherited phenomenon, as describe above, already the "gorilla is in the room" the expectations are unlikely to be met. It is simply too much to ask of President Obama given the realities of the moribund economy and the expansive unfinished business left over by President Bush to meet the expectations of restoring the battered American image abroad. There are opportunities to return to traditional foreign policy values, namely multilateralism. Until there are a series of major multilateral agreements that are not just signed by President Obama but ratified by the Senate, then the aforementioned measures, and others like them, will be simply viewed as window dressing.

In order to be successful in the foreign policy arena President Obama will not only have to survive the historic Democratic dilemma but find a way to defeat it. Carter failed and so too did Clinton. What are the prospects for Obama? With history as the central measure the prospects for President Obama's successful management of the Democratic dilemma are not promising.

Appendix A Executive Order Closing Guantanamo

On Thursday January 22, President Obama signed an executive order to close the prison at Guantanamo Bay. Read the full text:

By the authority vested in me as President by the Constitution and the laws of the United States of America, in order to effect the appropriate disposition of individuals currently detained by the Department of Defense at the Guantánamo Bay Naval Base (Guantánamo) and promptly to close detention facilities at Guantánamo, consistent with the national security and foreign policy interests of the United States and the interests of justice, I hereby order as follows:

Section 1. Definitions. As used in this order:

(a) "Common Article 3" means Article 3 of each of the Geneva Conventions.

(b) "Geneva Conventions" means:

  (i) The Convention for the Amelioration of the Condition of the Wounded and Sick in Armed Forces in the Field, August 12, 1949 (6 UST 3114);

  (ii) The Convention for the Amelioration of the Condition of Wounded, Sick and Shipwrecked Members of Armed Forces at Sea, August 12, 1949 (6 UST 3217);

  (iii) The Convention Relative to the Treatment of Prisoners of War, August 12, 1949 (6 UST 3316); and

  (iv) The Convention Relative to the Protection of Civilian Persons in Time of War, August 12, 1949 (6 UST 3516).

(c) "Individuals currently detained at Guantánamo" and "individuals covered by this order" mean individuals currently detained by the Department of Defense in facilities at the Guantánamo Bay Naval Base whom the Department of Defense has ever determined to be, or treated as, enemy combatants.

Sec. 2. Findings.

(a) Over the past 7 years, approximately 800 individuals whom the Department of Defense has ever determined to be, or treated as, enemy combatants have been detained at Guantánamo. The Federal Government has moved more than 500 such detainees from Guantánamo, either by returning them to their home country or by releasing or transferring them to a third country. The Department of Defense has determined that a number of the individuals currently detained at Guantánamo are eligible for such transfer or release.

(b) Some individuals currently detained at Guantánamo have been there for more than 6 years, and most have been detained for at least 4 years. In view of the significant concerns raised by these detentions, both within the United States and internationally, prompt and appropriate disposition of the individuals currently detained at Guantánamo and closure of the facilities in which they are detained would further the national security and foreign policy interests of the United States and the interests of justice. Merely closing the facilities without promptly determining the appropriate disposition of the individuals detained would not adequately serve those interests. To the extent practicable, the prompt and appropriate disposition of the individuals detained at Guantánamo should precede the closure of the detention facilities at Guantánamo.

(c) The individuals currently detained at Guantánamo have the constitutional privilege of the writ of habeas corpus. Most of those individuals have filed petitions for a writ of habeas corpus in Federal court challenging the lawfulness of their detention.

(d) It is in the interests of the United States that the executive branch undertake a prompt and thorough review of the factual and legal bases for the continued detention of all individuals currently held at Guantánamo, and of whether their continued detention is in the national security and foreign policy interests of the United States and in the interests of justice. The unusual circumstances associated with detentions at Guantánamo require a comprehensive interagency review.

(e) New diplomatic efforts may result in an appropriate disposition of a substantial number of individuals currently detained at Guantánamo.

(f) Some individuals currently detained at Guantánamo may have committed offenses for which they should be prosecuted. It is in the interests of the United States to review whether and how any such individuals can and should be prosecuted.

(g) It is in the interests of the United States that the executive branch conduct a prompt and thorough review of the circumstances of the individuals currently detained at Guantánamo who have been charged with offenses before military commissions pursuant to the Military Commissions Act of 2006, Public Law 109-366, as well as of the military commission process more generally.

Sec. 3. Closure of Detention Facilities at Guantánamo. The detention facilities at Guantánamo for individuals covered by this order shall be closed as soon as practicable, and no later than 1 year from the date of this order. If any individuals covered by this order remain in detention at Guantánamo at the time of closure of those detention facilities, they shall be returned to their home country, released, transferred to a third country, or transferred to another United States detention facility in a manner consistent with law and the national security and foreign policy interests of the United States.

Sec. 4. Immediate Review of All Guantánamo Detentions.

(a) Scope and Timing of Review. A review of the status of each individual currently detained at Guantánamo (Review) shall commence immediately.

(b) Review Participants. The Review shall be conducted with the full cooperation and participation of the following officials:

(1) the Attorney General, who shall coordinate the Review;

(2) the Secretary of Defense;

(3) the Secretary of State;

(4) the Secretary of Homeland Security;

(5) the Director of National Intelligence;

(6) the Chairman of the Joint Chiefs of Staff; and

(7) other officers or full-time or permanent part-time employees of the United States, including employees with intelligence, counterterrorism, military, and legal expertise, as determined by the Attorney General, with the concurrence of the head of the department or agency concerned.

(c) Operation of Review. The duties of the Review participants shall include the following:

(1) Consolidation of Detainee Information. The Attorney General shall, to the extent reasonably practicable, and in coordination with the other Review participants, assemble all information in the possession of the Federal Government that pertains to any individual currently detained at Guantánamo and that is relevant to determining the proper disposition of any such individual. All executive branch departments and agencies shall promptly comply with any request of the Attorney General to provide information in their possession or control pertaining to any such individual. The Attorney General may seek further information relevant to the Review from any source.

(2) Determination of Transfer. The Review shall determine, on a rolling basis and as promptly as possible with respect to the individuals currently detained at Guantánamo, whether it is possible to transfer or release the individuals consistent with the national security and foreign policy interests more of the United States and, if so, whether and how the Secretary of Defense may effect their transfer or release. The Secretary of Defense, the Secretary of State,

and, as appropriate, other Review participants shall work to effect promptly the release or transfer of all individuals for whom release or transfer is possible.

(3) Determination of Prosecution. In accordance with United States law, the cases of individuals detained at Guantánamo not approved for release or transfer shall be evaluated to determine whether the Federal Government should seek to prosecute the detained individuals for any offenses they may have committed, including whether it is feasible to prosecute such individuals before a court established pursuant to Article III of the United States Constitution, and the Review participants shall in turn take the necessary and appropriate steps based on such determinations.

(4) Determination of Other Disposition. With respect to any individuals currently detained at Guantánamo whose disposition is not achieved under paragraphs (2) or (3) of this subsection, the Review shall select lawful means, consistent with the national security and foreign policy interests of the United States and the interests of justice, for the disposition of such individuals. The appropriate authorities shall promptly implement such dispositions.

(5) Consideration of Issues Relating to Transfer to the United States. The Review shall identify and consider legal, logistical, and security issues relating to the potential transfer of individuals currently detained at Guantánamo to facilities within the United States, and the Review participants shall work with the Congress on any legislation that may be appropriate.

Sec. 5. Diplomatic Efforts. The Secretary of State shall expeditiously pursue and direct such negotiations and diplomatic efforts with foreign governments as are necessary and appropriate to implement this order.

Sec. 6. Humane Standards of Confinement. No individual currently detained at Guantánamo shall be held in the custody or under the effective control of any officer, employee, or other agent of the United States Government, or at a facility owned, operated, or controlled by a department or agency of the United States, except in conformity with all applicable laws governing the conditions of such confinement, including Common Article 3 of the Geneva Conventions. The Secretary of Defense shall immediately undertake a review of the conditions of detention at Guantánamo to ensure full compliance with this directive. Such review shall be completed within 30 days and any necessary corrections shall be implemented immediately thereafter.

Sec. 7. Military Commissions. The Secretary of Defense shall immediately take steps sufficient to ensure that during the pendency of the Review described in section 4 of this order, no charges are sworn, or referred to a military more commission under the Military Commissions Act of 2006 and the Rules for Military Commissions, and that all proceedings of such military commissions to which charges have been referred but in which no judgment has been rendered, and all proceedings pending in the United States Court of Military Commission Review, are halted.

Sec. 8. General Provisions.

(a) Nothing in this order shall prejudice the authority of the Secretary of Defense to determine the disposition of any detainees not covered by this order.

(b) This order shall be implemented consistent with applicable law and subject to the availability of appropriations.

This order is not intended to, and does not, create any right or benefit, substantive or procedural, enforceable at law or in equity by any party against the United States, its departments, agencies, or entities, its officers, employees, or agents, or any other person.

BARACK OBAMA
THE WHITE HOUSE,
January 22, 2009.

Appendix B-Executive Order Ensuring Lawful Interrogations

By the authority vested in me by the Constitution and the laws of the United States of America, in order to improve the effectiveness of human intelligence gathering, to promote the safe, lawful, and humane treatment of individuals in United States custody and of United States personnel who are detained in armed conflicts, to ensure compliance with the treaty obligations of the United States, including the Geneva Conventions, and to take care that the laws of the United States are faithfully executed, I hereby order as follows:

Section 1. Revocation. Executive Order 13440 of July 20, 2007, is revoked. All executive directives, orders, and regulations inconsistent with this order, including but not limited to those issued to or by the Central Intelligence Agency (CIA) from September 11, 2001, to January 20, 2009, concerning detention or the interrogation of detained individuals, are revoked to the extent of their inconsistency with this order. Heads of departments and agencies shall take all necessary steps to ensure that all directives, orders, and regulations of their respective departments or agencies are consistent with this order. Upon request, the Attorney General shall provide guidance about which directives, orders, and regulations are inconsistent with this order.

Sec. 2. Definitions. As used in this order:

(a) "Army Field Manual 2 22.3" means FM 2-22.3, Human Intelligence Collector Operations, issued by the Department of the Army on September 6, 2006.

(b) "Army Field Manual 34-52" means FM 34-52, Intelligence Interrogation, issued by the Department of the Army on May 8, 1987.

(c) "Common Article 3"means Article 3 of each of the Geneva Conventions.

(d) "Convention Against Torture" means the Convention Against Torture and Other Cruel, Inhuman or Degrading Treatment or Punishment, December 10, 1984, 1465 U.N.T.S. 85, S. Treaty Doc. No. 100 20 (1988).

(e) "Geneva Conventions" means:

(i) The Convention for the Amelioration of the Condition of the Wounded and Sick in Armed Forces in the Field, August 12, 1949 (6 UST 3114);

(ii) The Convention for the Amelioration of the Condition of Wounded, Sick and Shipwrecked Members of Armed Forces at Sea, August 12, 1949 (6 UST 3217);

(iii) The Convention Relative to the Treatment of Prisoners of War, August 12, 1949 (6 UST 3316); and

(iv) The Convention Relative to the Protection of Civilian Persons in Time of War, August 12, 1949 (6 UST 3516).

(f) "Treated humanely," "violence to life and person," "murder of all kinds," "mutilation," "cruel treatment," "torture," "outrages upon personal dignity," and "humiliating and degrading treatment" refer to, and have the same meaning as, those same terms in Common Article 3.

(g) The terms "detention facilities" and "detention facility" in section 4(a) of this order do not refer to facilities used only to hold people on a short-term, transitory basis.

Sec. 3. Standards and Practices for Interrogation of Individuals in the Custody or Control of the United States in Armed Conflicts.

(a) Common Article 3 Standards as a Minimum Baseline. Consistent with the requirements of the Federal torture statute, 18 U.S.C. 2340 2340A, section 1003 of the Detainee Treatment Act of 2005, 42 U.S.C. 2000dd, the Convention Against Torture, Common Article 3, and other laws regulating the treatment and interrogation of individuals detained in any armed conflict, such persons shall in all circumstances be treated humanely and shall not be subjected to violence to life and person (including murder of all kinds, mutilation, cruel treatment, and torture), nor to outrages upon personal dignity (including humiliating and degrading treatment), whenever such individuals are in the custody or under the effective control of an officer, employee, or other agent of the United States Government or detained within a facility owned, operated, or controlled by a department or agency of the United States.

(b) Interrogation Techniques and Interrogation-Related Treatment. Effective immediately, an individual in the custody or under the effective control of an officer, employee, or other agent of the United States Government, or detained within a facility owned, operated, or controlled by a department or agency of the United States, in any armed conflict, shall not be subjected to any interrogation technique or approach, or any treatment related to interrogation, that is not authorized by and listed in Army Field Manual 2 22.3 (Manual). Interrogation techniques, approaches, and treatments described in the Manual shall be implemented strictly in accord with the principles, processes, conditions, and limitations the Manual prescribes. Where processes required by the Manual, such as a requirement of approval by specified Department of Defense officials, are inapposite to a department or an agency other than the Department of Defense, such a department or agency shall use processes that are substantially equivalent to the processes the Manual prescribes for the Department of Defense. Nothing in this section shall preclude the Federal Bureau of

Investigation, or other Federal law enforcement agencies, from continuing to use authorized, non-coercive techniques of interrogation that are designed to elicit voluntary statements and do not involve the use of force, threats, or promises.

(c) Interpretations of Common Article 3 and the Army Field Manual. From this day forward, unless the Attorney General with appropriate consultation provides further guidance, officers, employees, and other agents of the United States Government may, in conducting interrogations, act in reliance upon Army Field Manual 2 22.3, but may not, in conducting interrogations, rely upon any interpretation of the law governing interrogation—including interpretations of Federal criminal laws, the Convention Against Torture, Common Article 3, Army Field Manual 2 22.3, and its predecessor document, Army Field Manual 34-52 issued by the Department of Justice between September 11, 2001, and January 20, 2009.

Sec. 4. Prohibition of Certain Detention Facilities, and Red Cross Access to Detained Individuals.

(a) CIA Detention. The CIA shall close as expeditiously as possible any detention facilities that it currently operates and shall not operate any such detention facility in the future.

(b) International Committee of the Red Cross Access to Detained Individuals. All departments and agencies of the Federal Government shall provide the International Committee of the Red Cross with notification of, and timely access to, any individual detained in any armed conflict in the custody or under the effective control of an officer, employee, or other agent of the United States Government or detained within a facility owned, operated, or controlled by a department or agency of the United States Government, consistent with Department of Defense regulations and policies.

Sec. 5. Special Interagency Task Force on Interrogation and Transfer Policies.

(a) Establishment of Special Interagency Task Force. There shall be established a Special Task Force on Interrogation and Transfer Policies (Special Task Force) to review interrogation and transfer policies.

(b) Membership. The Special Task Force shall consist of the following members, or their designees:

(i) the Attorney General, who shall serve as Chair;

(ii) the Director of National Intelligence, who shall serve as Co-Vice-Chair;

(iii) the Secretary of Defense, who shall serve as Co-Vice-Chair;

(iv) the Secretary of State;

(v) the Secretary of Homeland Security;

(vi) the Director of the Central Intelligence Agency;

(vii) the Chairman of the Joint Chiefs of Staff; and

(viii)   other officers or full-time or permanent part time employees of the United States, as determined by the Chair, with the concurrence of the head of the department or agency concerned.

(c) Staff. The Chair may designate officers and employees within the Department of Justice to serve as staff to support the Special Task Force. At the request of the Chair, officers and employees from other departments or agencies may serve on the Special Task Force with the concurrence of the head of the department or agency that employ such individuals. Such staff must be officers or full-time or permanent part-time employees of the United States. The Chair shall designate an officer or employee of the Department of Justice to serve as the Executive Secretary of the Special Task Force.

(d) Operation. The Chair shall convene meetings of the Special Task Force, determine its agenda, and direct its work. The Chair may establish and direct subgroups of the Special Task Force, consisting exclusively of members of the Special Task Force, to deal with particular subjects.

(e) Mission. The mission of the Special Task Force shall be:

(i)   To study and evaluate whether the interrogation practices and techniques in Army Field Manual 2 22.3, when employed by departments or agencies outside the military, provide an appropriate means of acquiring the intelligence necessary to protect the Nation, and, if warranted, to recommend any additional or different guidance for other departments or agencies; and

(ii) to study and evaluate the practices of transferring individuals to other nations in order to ensure that such practices comply with the domestic laws, international obligations, and policies of the United States and do not result in the transfer of individuals to other nations to face torture or otherwise for the purpose, or with the effect, of undermining or circumventing the commitments or obligations of the United States to ensure the humane treatment of individuals in its custody or control.

(f) Administration. The Special Task Force shall be established for administrative purposes within the Department of Justice and the Department of Justice shall, to the extent permitted by law and subject to the availability of appropriations, provide administrative support and funding for the Special Task Force.

(g) Recommendations. The Special Task Force shall provide a report to the President, through the Assistant to the President for National Security Affairs and the Counsel to the President, on the matters set forth in subsection (d) within 180 days of the date of this order, unless the Chair determines that an extension is necessary.

(h) Termination. The Chair shall terminate the Special Task Force upon the completion of its duties.

Sec. 6. Construction with Other Laws. Nothing in this order shall be construed to affect the obligations of officers, employees, and other agents of the United States Government to comply with all pertinent laws and treaties of the United States governing detention and interrogation, including but not limited to: the Fifth and Eighth Amendments to the United States Constitution;

the Federal torture statute, 18 U.S.C. 2340 2340A; the War Crimes Act, 18 U.S.C. 2441; the Federal assault statute, 18 U.S.C. 113; the Federal maiming statute, 18 U.S.C. 114; the Federal "stalking" statute, 18 U.S.C. 2261A; articles 93, 124, 128, and 134 of the Uniform Code of Military Justice, 10 U.S.C. 893, 924, 928, and 934; section 1003 of the Detainee Treatment Act of 2005, 42 U.S.C. 2000dd; section 6(c) of the Military Commissions Act of 2006, Public Law 109 366; the Geneva Conventions; and the Convention Against Torture. Nothing in this order shall be construed to diminish any rights that any individual may have under these or other laws and treaties. This order is not intended to, and does not create any right or benefit, substantive or procedural, enforceable at law or in equity against the United States, its departments, agencies, or other entities, its officers or employees, or any other person.

Barack Obama
The White House,
January 22, 2009

(Endnotes)

1 Senator Barack Obama, "The American Moment," April 23, 2007. Remarks delivered before The Chicago Council on Global Affairs. http://www.thechicagocouncil.org/dynamic_page. php?id=64. The site was accessed on November 12, 2008.

2 Ibid.

3 Barack Obama, "Renewing American Leadership," *Foreign Affairs*, July/August 2007. http:// www.foreignaffairs.org/20070701faessay86401/barack-obama/renewing-american-leadership.html?mode=print. The site was accessed on November 12, 2008.

4 Amitai Etzioni, "Obama's Vacuous Foreign Policy," July 6, 2007. http://www.huffingtonpost. com/amitai-etzioni/obamas-vacuous-foreign-p_b_55260.html. The site was accessed on November 12, 2008.

5 Jeff Zeleny, "Obama Outlines His Foreign Policy Views," *New York Times*, April 24, 2007. http://www.nytimes.com/2007/04/24/us/politics/24obama.html. The site was accessed on November 12, 2008.

6 Jim Malone, "US Democratic Presidential Contenders Clash Over Foreign Policy," Voice of America, August 9, 2007. http://www.voanews.com/english/archive/2007-08/2007-08-09-voa48.cfm. The site was accessed on November 12, 2008.

7 "Below the Beltway," (Blog) February 29, 2008. http://belowthebeltway.com/2008/02/29/ hillary-clinton-plays-the-fear-card/. The site was accessed on November 13, 2008.

8 "Barack Obama's Own 3 am Phone Ringing Ad," Youtube, March 21, 2008. http://www. youtube.com/watch?v=9BvyF351RS8. The site was accessed on November 13, 2008.

9 "McCain, Obama Election Blitz on Final Lap," ABCNews, Nov 2, 2008. http://www.abc. net.au/news/stories/2008/11/02/2407770.htm?section=world. The site was accessed on November 13, 2008.

10 Elisabeth Bumiller, "McCain Raps Obama Again on Iraq, Preconditions," *New York Times*, May 28, 2008. http://thecaucus.blogs.nytimes.com/2008/05/28/mccain-raps-obama-again-on-iraq-preconditions/. The site was accessed on November 13, 2008.

11 Ibid.

12 Jeffery Zelleny, "Obama Plans Trip Pre-Election Day Visit to Iraq and Afghanistan," *New York Times*, June 16, 2008. http://thecaucus.blogs.nytimes.com/2008/06/16/obama-plans-trip-pre-election-day-visit-to-iraq-and-afghanistan/. The site was accessed on November 14, 2008.

13 Elisabeth Bummiller, "A Cast of 300 Advises Obama on Foreign Policy," *New York Times*, July 18, 2008. http://www.nytimes.com/2008/07/18/us/politics/18advisers.html?_r=1&hp=&pagewanted=print. The site was accessed on November 14, 2008.

14 Andrew Romano, "HIRSH: 'Ich bin ein Commander,'" *Newsweek*, July 18, 2008. http://blog.newsweek.com/blogs/stumper/archive/2008/07/18/hirsh-ich-bin-ein-commander.aspx. The site was accessed on November 14, 2008.

15 "Obama makes first trip to Afghanistan," *CNN*, July 19, 2008. http://edition.cnn.com/2008/POLITICS/07/19/obama.afghanistan/index.html. The site was accessed on November 14, 2008.

16 "Iraq Unsure How to Greet Obama," *Time*, July 20, 2008. http://www.time.com/time/world/article/0,8599,1824787,00.html. The site was accessed on November 15, 2008.

17 "Obama Says Nuclear Iran Poses "Grave Threat," *Reuters*, July 23, 2008. http://www.reuters.com/article/politicsNews/idUSL23104041320080723. The site was accessed on November 15, 2008.

18 Michael Finnegan and Richard Boudreaux, "Barack Obama Meets with Leaders in Israel and Palestinian Territories," *LosAngelesTime*s, July 24, 2008. http://articles.latimes.com/2008/jul/24/nation/na-obamatrip24. The site was accessed on November 15, 2008.

19 Bradley Burston and Raphael Ahren, "GA Special Report / Peres to Obama: To Help Israel, be a Great President for the US," *Haaretz*, July 23, 2008. http://www.haaretz.com/hasen/spages/1038121.html. The site was accessed on November 15, 2008.

20 "Majority of Voters Unimpressed by Obama's Foreign Trip: Poll," August 10, 2008. http://www.indiapost.com/article/usnews/3522/. The site was accessed on November 15, 2008.

21 Laura Manning, "Obama Statement on Conflict in Georgia," August 11, 2008. http://my.barackobama.com/page/community/post/laurinmanning/gG5bh2. The site was accessed on November 15, 2008.

22 Abigail Hauslohner, "Team Obama Calls McCain's Georgia Stance 'Belligerent,' Yet 'Roughly The Same' As Theirs," *NationalReviewonline*, August 18, 2008. http://campaignspot.nationalreview.com/post/?q=NDE0ZjA3MmQ2NzhkYzFiNTAyZTJhNDRlOTcwOTgwN2M=. The site was accessed on November 15, 2008.

23 "Transcript of First Presidential Debate," *CNN*, October 14, 2008. http://edition.cnn.com/2008/POLITICS/09/26/debate.mississippi.transcript/. The site was accessed on November 15, 2008.

24 Ibid.

25 Ibid.

26 Ibid.

27 Ivo H. Daadler and James M. Lindsay, *America Unbound: The Bush Revolution in Foreign Policy* (Washington, DC: Brookings Institution Press, 2003), 13.

28 Henry J. Steiner, Philip Alston, Ryan Goodman, *International Human Rights in Context: Law, Politics, Morals* (New York: Oxford University Press, 2007), 296.

29 Aziz Huq, "Undoing the Bush Legacy," *The Nation*, February 8, 2008. http://www.thenation.com/doc/20080225/huq. The site was accessed on November 16, 2008.

30 Susan Sachs, "A Nation At War: International Reaction; Crowds Protest Iraq War In Cities Around World," *New York Times*, March 22, 2003. http://query.nytimes.com/gst/fullpage.html?res=9806E0DD1F31F931A15750C0A9659C8B63&sec=&spon=&pagewanted=2. The site was accessed on November 16, 2008.

31 "Outrage at 'Old Europe' Remarks," *BBC*, January 23, 2003. http://news.bbc.co.uk/2/hi/europe/2687403.stm. The site was accessed on November 16, 2008.

32 Zbigniew Brezezinski, *Second Chance: Three Presidents and the Crisis of American Superpower*, Paperback Edition (New York, Basic Books, 2007), 184-185.

33 Ellen McGirt, "The Brand Called Obama," *Fast Company*, March 19, 2008. http://cgrnbc.googlepages.com/TheBrandCalledObama.pdf. The site was accessed on November 16, 2008.

34 Fred Kaplan, "Karen Hughes Sells Brand America," *Slate*, March 15, 2005. http://www.slate.com/id/2114854/. The site was accessed on November 17, 2008.

35 Jimmy Carter, "Human Rights and Foreign Policy," Commencement Speech Given at Notre Dame University, June 1997. http://www.teachingamericanhistory.org/library/index.asp?document=727. The site was accessed on November 17, 2008.

36 Itai Nartzizenfield Sneh, "The Future Almost Arrived: Why and How Jimmy Carter Failed to Change US Foreign Policy," Nathan Hale Foreign Policy Society Working Paper Series. http://www.foreignpolicysociety.org/workingpapers/WP8--Sneh.pdf. The site was accessed on November 17, 2008.

37 'A New Dawn of American Leadership is at Hand,'" *Evening Standard*, November 10, 2008. http://www.thisislondon.co.uk/standard/article-23582467-details/'A+new+dawn+of+American+leadership+is+at+hand'/article.do. The site was accessed on November 17, 2008.

38 Remarks of Senator Barack Obama to the Chicago Council on Global Affairs, April 23, 2007. http://my.barackobama.com/page/content/fpccga/. The site was accessed on November 17, 2008.

39 Jonathan Steele, "Obama Says He'll Reshape US Foreign Policy, But Can He?" *The Guardian*, May 14 2008. http://www.guardian.co.uk/commentisfree/2008/may/14/barackobama.usforeignpolicy. The site was accessed on November 17, 2008.

40 Ethan Bronner, "For Many Abroad, An Ideal Renewed," *International Herald Tribune*, November 5, 2008. http://www.iht.com/articles/2008/11/05/america/05global.php. The site was accessed on November 17, 2008.

41 Ibid.

42 Edward Cohen, "Obama's Foreign Policy," *Diplomat*, February 7, 2007. http://www.the-diplomat.com/article.aspx?aeid=3210. The site was accessed on November 18, 2008.

43 Christopher Preble, "Barack Obama's Exceptionalism," Cato Institution. http://www.cato.org/pub_display.php?pub_id=8380. The site was accessed on November 18, 2008.

44 Strobe Talbott, "How the US Can Fix its Damaged Reputation Abroad." Speigel Online International, October 13, 2008. http://www.spiegel.de/international/0,1518,583723,00.html. The site was accessed on November 18, 2008.

45 "Improving the United States Image Abroad," General Accounting Office, 2009 Congressional and Presidential Transition. http://www.gao.gov/transition_2009/urgent/diplomacy-broadcasting.php. The site was accessed on November 18, 2008.

46 Ibid.

47 R.S. Zaharna, "The US Credibility Deficit," *Foreign Policy in Focus*, December 13, 2006. http://www.fpif.org/fpiftxt/3796. The site was accessed on November 18, 2008.

48 Merle D. Kellerhals Jr., "Obama Emphasizes Multilateral US Foreign Policymaking," America.gov, July 25, 2008.http://www.america.gov/st/elections08-english/2008/July/2008072516 2819dmslahrellek0.840069.html. The site was accessed on November 20, 2008.

49 Spencer Ackerman, "The Obama Doctrine," *The American Prospect*, March 24, 2008. http://www.prospect.org/cs/articles?article=the_obama_doctrine. The site was accessed on November 20, 2008.

50 Ibid.

51 Barack Obama, "Renewing American Leadership," *Foreign Affairs*, July/August 2007. http://www.foreignaffairs.org/20070701faessay86401/barack-obama/renewing-american-leadership.html. The site was accessed on November 20, 2008.

52 Ibid.

53 Jay Newton-Small, "Obama's Foreign-Policy Problem," *Time*. http://www.time.com/time/politics/article/0,8599,1695803,00.html. The site was accessed on November 20, 2008.

54 Remarks of President-elect Barack Obama, Announcement of National Security Team, December 1st, 2008, Chicago, IL. http://change.gov/newsroom/entry/the_national_security_team/. The site was accessed on November 21, 2008.

55 Jim Lobe, Diplomacy, Multilateralism Stressed by Obama Team," December 2, 2008. http://www.antiwar.com/lobe/?articleid=13843. The site was accessed on November 21, 2008.

56 Ibid.

57 Jim Lobe, "Obama's Foreign Policy-No Sharp Break From Bush," *Inter Press Service*, November 11, 2008. http://www.rense.com/general84/oob.htm. The site was accessed on November 21, 2008.

58 Bernard Gwertzman, "Obama's First Priority Should Be The Economy," Council On Foreign Relations, November 7, 2008. http://www.newsweek.com/id/168047?tid=relatedcl. The site was accessed on November 21, 2008.

59 Seymour M. Hersh, "Preparing The Battlefield," *The New Yorker*, July 7, 2008. http://www.newyorker.com/reporting/2008/07/07/080707fa_fact_hersh. The site was accessed on March 19, 2009.

60 Lobe, "Obama's Foreign Policy-No Sharp Break From Bush."

61 Ibid.

62 "Transcript of Obama's Message in Celebration of Nowruz," *Wall Street Journal*, March 20, 2009. http://online.wsj.com/article/SB123752091165792573.html?mod=googlenews_wsj. The site was accessed on March 22, 2009.

63 Ian Black "Iran Gives Cautious Welcome to Barack Obama Video Message," *The Guardian*, March 20, 2009. http://www.guardian.co.uk/world/2009/mar/20/barack-obama-iran-message. The site was accessed on March 23, 2009.

64 David Rothkopf, *Running the World: The Inside Story of the National Security Council and the Architects of American Power* (New York: Public Affairs, 2004), 404.

65 Ibid.

66 Ibid.

67 The EU's Contribution to Afghanistan's Reconstruction Process, June 29, 2008. http://www.europa-eu-un.org/articles/en/article_1075_en.htm. The site was accessed on March 23, 2009.

68 "Obama Calls Situation in Afghanistan 'Urgent,'" *CNN*, July 21, 2008. http://www.cnn.com/2008/POLITICS/07/20/obama.afghanistan/. The site was accessed on March 23, 2009.

69 For more on this point see, Robert Dallek, Franklin D. Roosevelt and American Foreign Policy, 1932-1945, 2nd Edition (Oxford: Oxford University Press, 1995), 38-43 and Carl-Ludwig Holtfrerich, The Roosevelt's and Foreign Trade: Foreign Economic Policies Under Theodore and Franklin Roosevelt (Institute of Berlin, 1986).

70 Kenneth I. Juster and Simon Lazarus, *Making Economic Policy: An Assessment of the National Economic Council* (Washington, DC: Brookings Institution Press, 1997).

71 Michael Mandelbaum, "Foreign Policy as Social Work," *Foreign Affairs*, January/February 1996. http://www.foreignaffairs.org/19960101faessay4169/michael-mandelbaum/foreign-policy-as-social-work.html?mode=print. The site was accessed on March 23, 2009.

72 Ibid.

73 Jeff Taylor, "More Muscular Interventionism, The Foreign Policy of Barack Obama," *Counterpunch Weekend Edition*, June 23/24, 2007. http://www.counterpunch.org/taylor06232007.html. The site was accessed on March 23, 2009.

74 "Obama: Clinton Would Continue "Bush Doctrine." *ABC News*, July 26, 2007. http://blogs.abcnews.com/politicalradar/2007/07/obama-clinton-w.html. The site was accessed on November 22, 2008.

75 Transcript, Senator Barack Obama, "The World Beyond Iraq," March 19, 2008. http://my.barackobama.com/page/community/post/samgrahamfelsen/gGBFrl. The site was accessed on November 22, 2008.

76 A National Security Strategy of Engagement and Enlargement, The White House, February 1996. http://www.fas.org/spp/military/docops/national/1996stra.htm#II. The site was accessed on November 22, 2008.

77 Ibid.

78 Ibid.

79 Benjamin Schwarz, "The Vision Thing: Sustaining the Unsustainable," *World Policy Journal*, 1994, Vol. 11, 1994. http://www.questia.com/googleScholar.qst;jsessionid=JGhJMh4nYy2stQ61ppHTykLYG0svpKJs0p73TWQfJf8YfXn2yVb1!-605221181?docId=94487709. The site was accessed on November 22, 2008.

80 Robert Manning and Patrick Clawson, "The Clinton Doctrine," *Wall Street Journal*, December 29, 1997. http://www.washingtoninstitute.org/templateC06.php?CID=413. The site was accessed on November 23, 2008.

81 The National Security Strategy, The White House, September 2002. http://www.whitehouse.gov/nsc/nss/2002/index.html. The site was accessed on November 23, 2008.

82 Joseph S. Nye, Jr., "Transformational Leadership and U.S. Grand Strategy," *Foreign Affairs*, July/August 2006. http://www.foreignaffairs.org/20060701faessay85411/joseph-s-nye-jr/transformational-leadership-and-u-s-grand-strategy.html. The site was accessed on November 23, 2008.

83 Shawn Brimley, "A Grand Strategy of Sustainment," March 25, 2008. http://smallwarsjournal.com/blog/2008/03/a-grand-strategy-of-sustainmen/. The site was accessed on November 23, 2008.

84 Fareed Zakaria, "Wanted: A New Grand Strategy," *Newsweek*, November 29, 2008. http://www.newsweek.com/id/171249. The site was accessed on November 30, 2008.

85 Ibid.

86 Matt Bondy, "Obama's Global Strategy Lacks Vision," March 31, 2008. http://news.guelphmercury.com/article/311616

87 Thomas P.M. Barnett, "The Obama Presidency: A Grand Strategy Agenda," *World Politics Review*, November 10, 2008. http://www.worldpoliticsreview.com/article.aspx?id=2894. The site was accessed on November 30, 2008.

88 Ibid.

89 Dave Schuler, "Wanted: A Grand Strategy (Updated)," Outside The Beltway, December 2, 2008. http://www.outsidethebeltway.com/archives/wanted_a_grand_strategy/. The site was accessed on November 30, 2008.

90 Ibid.

91 David Brooks, "Continuity We Can Believe In," *New York Times*, December 1, 2008. http://www.nytimes.com/2008/12/02/opinion/02brooks.html?_r=1&ref=opinion. The site was accessed on November 30, 2008.

92 Mandy Castle, "Jane's Looks at Obama's Priorities on Taking Over the U.S. Presidency," *Janes*, November 5, 2008. http://www.janes.com/media/releases/pc081105_2.shtml. The site was accessed on November 30, 2008.

93 Ralph Peters, "Perilous Theories, Obama's Foreign Policy Trap," *The New York Post*, December 8, 2008. http://www.nypost.com/seven/12082008/postopinion/opedcolumnists/perilous_theories_143189.htm. The site was accessed on November 30, 2008.

94 Bruce D. Berkowitz, "A National Security Strategy of Engagement and Enlargement" (Book Review), *Orbis*, Spring 1997. http://findarticles.com/p/articles/mi_m0365/is_n2_v41/ai_19416344/pg_2. The site was accessed on November 30, 2008.

95 Barry Posen, "The Case for Restraint," *The American Interest*, November-December 2007.

96 Steve Clemons, "Grand Strategy vs. Crisis Management and Incrementalism," Washington Note, June 11, 2008. http://www.thewashingtonnote.com/archives/2008/06/mitchell_reiss/. The site was accessed on November 30, 2008.

97 Swaraaj Chauhan, "India Celebrates Barack Obama Win," The Moderate Voice, November 5, 2008. http://themoderatevoice.com/24076/india-celebrates-barack-obama-win/. The site was accessed on March 2, 2009.

98 Ibid.

99 "India is 'Top Priority' for Barack Obama," *South Asian Post*, October 30 2008. http://www.southasianpost.com/portal2/c1ee8c441d4a4790011d4ef802b101d9_India_is__top_priority__for_Barack_Obama.do.html. The site was accessed on March 2, 2009.

100 Ibid.

101 Anwar Iqbal, "US Should Help Resolve Kashmir Issue: Obama: 'Militants, Not India, Biggest threat to Pakistan.'" November 3, 2008. http://www.dawn.com/2008/11/03/top1.htm. The site was accessed on March 2, 2009.

102 C. Raja Mohan, "Barack Obama's Kashmir Thesis!" *ExpressIndia*, November 3, 2008. http://www.expressindia.com/latest-news/Barack-Obamas-Kashmir-thesis/380615/

103 Lisa Curtis and Walter Lohman, "Stiffening Pakistan's Resolve Against Terrorism: A Memo to President-elect Obama," *Heritage Foundation Special Report*, December 18, 2008. http://www.heritage.org/Research/AsiaandthePacific/sr34.cfm. The site was accessed on March 2, 2009.

104 Arvind Panagariya, *India: The Emerging Giant*. Oxford: Oxford University Press, 2008.

105 Top 10 Global Economic Challenges Facing America's 44th President of the United States. Brookings Institution, 2008-2009. http://www.brookings.edu/reports/2008/~/media/Files/rc/reports/2008/10_global_economics_top_ten/top_ten_2008.pdf. The site was accessed on March 2, 2009.

106 Ibid.

107 Jonathan Krim, "Intel Chairman Says US Is Losing Edge," *Washington Post*, October 10, 2003, E01.

108 "Oil Maneuvers by China, India, Challenge US," ExpressIndia.com, July 20, 2005. http://www.expressindia.com/news/fullstory.php?newsid=51042. The site was accessed on March 2, 2009.

109 For more on this point, see Fareed Zakaria, *The Post-American World* (New York: W. W. Norton, 2008).

110 "US–India Strategic Economic Partnership," US-India CEO Forum, March 2006. http://planningcommission.nic.in/reports/genrep/USIndia.pdf. The site was accessed on March 3, 2009.

111 J. Michael McConnell Director of National Intelligence, DNI Annual Threat Assessment before the

Senate Select Committee on Intelligence, February 5, 2008. http://intelligence.senate.gov/080205/mcconnell.pdf. The site was accessed on March 3, 2009.

112 Ibid.

113 Senator Barack Obama, "The American Moment," April 23, 2007. http://www.thechicagocouncil.org/dynamic_page.php?id=64. The site was accessed on March 3, 2009.

114 Barack Obama, "Renewing American Leadership," *Foreign Affairs*, July/August 2007. http://www.foreignaffairs.org/20070701faessay86401/barack-obama/renewing-american-leadership.html?mode=print. The site was accessed on March 3, 2009.

115 Yuri Mamchur, "Medvedev Wants "Fresh Start" in US-Russia Relations, But Doesn't Start Fresh Himself," Russiablog, November 2008. http://www.russiablog.org/2008/11/medvedev_obama_fresh_start_us_russia_speech.php. The site was accessed on March 4, 2009.

116 Ibid.

117 'Meet the Press' Transcript for December 7, 2008. Transcript of the December 7, 2008 broadcast of *NBC*'s '*Meet the Press*,' featuring President-elect Barack Obama. http://www.msnbc.msn.com/id/28097635/from/ET/

118 "Obama and McCain Debate Russia," September 27, 2008. http://www.robertamsterdam.com/2008/09/obama_and_mccain_debate_russia.htm. The site was accessed on March 4, 2009.

119 "Time to Revisit Relations with Russia, Biden Says," America.gov. February 9, 2009. http://www.america.gov/st/peacesec-english/2009/February/20090209153734idybeekcm0.1029627.html. The site was accessed on March 12, 2009.

120 Jill Dougherty, "US Seeks to 'Reset' Relations with Russia," *CNN*, March 7, 2009. http://www.cnn.com/2009/WORLD/europe/03/07/us.russia/. The site was accessed on March 12, 2009.

121 Helene Cooper, "Russia Aims to Be High on Obama's Agenda," *New York Times*, November 7, 2008. http://www.nytimes.com/2008/11/08/world/europe/08russia.html. The site was accessed on March 13, 2009.

122 Alastair Gee, "How Tough-Talking Russia Sees Obama," *US News &World Report*, November 7, 2008. http://www.usnews.com/articles/news/world/2008/11/07/how-tough-talking-russia-sees-obama.html. The site was accessed on March 13, 2009.

123 Ibid.

124 "Barack Obama and Joe Biden: Protecting US Interests and Advancing American Values in our Relationship with China," May 23, 2007. http://www.chineseamericansforobama.com/factsheets/Obama's%20position%20on%20China.pdf. The site was accessed on March 13, 2009.

125 Ibid.

126 2007 Democratic Primary Debate. Sponsored by the *Des Moines Register*, December 13, 2007, Final Debate Before Iowa Caucus. http://www.ontheissues.org/2007_Dems_DMR.htm. The site was accessed on March 13, 2009.

127 Ibid.

128 "Barack Obama and Joe Biden: Technology." http://www.barackobama.com/issues/technology/. The site was accessed on December 23, 2008.

129 Frank Ching, Obama's China Policy, *The Korean Times*, March 13, 2009. http://www.koreatimes.co.kr/www/news/opinon/2008/12/171_35357.html. The site was accessed on March 13, 2009.

130 David C. Hendrickson, "The Curious Case of American Hegemony Imperial Aspirations and National Decline," *World Policy Journal*, Summer 2005, 10-11.

131 Military Power of the People's Republic of China, A Report to Congress Pursuant to the National Defense Authorization Act Fiscal Year 2000. http://www.dod.mil/pubs/pdfs/China%20Report%202006.pdf. The site was accessed on March 13, 2009.

132 Ibid.

133 Julian E. Barnes, "Chinese Threat Is Expanding, Pentagon Says," *Los Angeles Times*, May 24, 2006.

134 "China Fury at US Military Report," *BBC NewChannel*, March 26, 2009, http://news.bbc.co.uk/1/hi/world/asia-pacific/7965084.stm. The site was accessed on March 26, 2009.

135 Ibid.

136 Esther Pan, "The Scope of China's Military Threat," Council on Foreign Relations, June 2, 2006. http://www.cfr.org/publication/10824/. The site was accessed on March 26, 2009.

137 Hendrickson, "The Curious Case of American Hegemony Imperial Aspirations and National Decline."

138 "How Will Obama Approach China? The Plank," November 11, 2008. Responses by Perry Link, a China specialist and Chancellorial Chair for Teaching Across Disciplines at the University of California at Riverside. http://blogs.tnr.com/tnr/blogs/the_plank/archive/2008/12/11/how-will-obama-approach-china.aspx. The site was accessed on March 26, 2009.

139 "Barack Obama and Joe Biden: Protecting U.S. Interests and Advancing American Values in our Relationship with China," May 23, 2007.

140 Senator Barack Obama, "The American Moment," Chicago Council on Global Affairs, April 23, 2007. http://www.thechicagocouncil.org/dynamic_page.php?id=64. The site was accessed on March 26, 2009.

141 Barack Obama, "Renewing American Leadership," *Foreign Affairs*, July/August 2007. http://www.foreignaffairs.org/20070701faessay86401/barack-obama/renewing-american-leadership.html?mode=print. This site was accessed on January 2, 2009.

142 Robert Dreyfuss, "The Quagmire: As the Iraq War Drags on, it's Beginning to Look a Lot Like Vietnam," May 7, 2005. *Rolling Stone*. http://www.commondreams.org/views05/0507-23.htm. This site was accessed on January 2, 2009.

143 Bob Woodward, "Secret Reports Dispute White House Optimism," *Washington Post*, October 1, 2006, A1. http://www.washingtonpost.com/wp-dyn/content/article/2006/09/30/AR2006093000293_pf.html. This site was accessed on January 2, 2009.

144 Ibid,

145 "Bush Says Victory in Iraq Critical to Security of Civilized World," America.gov, September 2, 2006. http://www.america.gov/st/washfile-english/2006/September/20060902101029esnamfuak0.3611261.html. This site was accessed on January 3, 2009.

146 Jonathan Henry, "Why the Surge Worked," Strategy Page, January 28, 2008. http://www.strategypage.com/dls/articles/200812122042.asp. This site was accessed on January 4, 2009.

147 Illinois State Senator Barack Obama's Speech Against the Iraq War, October 2, 2002, The Federal Plaza in Chicago.

http://michael-miller.wiki.uml.edu/file/view/Obama+2002+against+war+in+Iraq.pdf. This site was accessed on January 4, 2009.

148 "A Way Forward in Iraq," Remarks of Senator Barack Obama at the Chicago Council on Global Affairs, November 20, 2006. http://usforeignpolicy.about.com/gi/dynamic/offsite. htm?zi=1/XJ&sdn=usforeignpolicy&cdn=newsissues&tm=168&gps=371_516_1276_6 04&f=21&su=p649.3.336.ip_&tt=11&bt=0&bts=0&zu=http%3A//obama.senate.gov/ speech/061120-a_way_forward_in_iraq/index.html.This site was accessed on January 4, 2009 This site was accessed on January 4, 2009.

149 Text of Senator Obama's Announcement, *New York Times*, February 10, 2007. http://www. nytimes.com/2007/02/10/us/politics/11obama-text.html. This site was accessed on January 4, 2009.

150 Note: Obama would make similar statement during a CNN/Nevada Democrat Party Democrat Presidential Candidate Debate, Las Vegas, Nevada on November 15, 2007. During that debate Obama the following comment: "But the overall strategy has failed, because we have not seen any change in behavior among Iraq's political leaders. And that is the essence of what we should be trying to do in Iraq. That's why I'm going to bring this war to a close. That's why we can get our combat troops out within 16 months." See, Transcript November 15, 2007 Democratic Debate. http://www.msnbc.msn.com/id/21836286/ page/14/

151 Senator Barack Obama, "The American Moment," The Chicago Council on Global Affairs, April 23, 2007. http://www.thechicagocouncil.org/dynamic_page.php?id=64. This site was accessed on January 5, 2009.

152 Transcript of Democratic Presidential Candidates Debate on September 26, 2007. http:// www.msnbc.msn.com/id/21013767/. This site was accessed on January 5, 2009.

153 Transcript, Senator Barack Obama, "The World Beyond Iraq," March 19, 2008. http:// my.barackobama.com/page/community/post/samgrahamfelsen/gGBFrl. This site was accessed on January 5, 2009.

154 Ibid.

155 Ibid.

156 Jason Linkins, "Obama Slams McCain, Strategy on Today," *The Huffington Post,* April 8, 2008. www.huffingtonpost.com/2008/04/08/obama-slams-mccain-iraq-s_n_95583. html?show_comment_id=12376262-32k. This site was accessed on January 5, 2009.

157 Kate Phillips, "War at Home: Bush's Iraq Troops Drawdown," *New York Times*, September 9, 2008. http://thecaucus.blogs.nytimes.com/2008/09/09/war-at-home-bushs-iraq-troops-drawdown/. This site was accessed on January 5, 2009.

158 Ibid.

159 Transcript of Second McCain, Obama Debate, *CNN*, October 7, 2007. http://www.cnn. com/2008/POLITICS/10/07/presidential.debate.transcript/index.html. This site was accessed on January 6, 2009.

160 William Rusher, "RUSHER: Democrats' Dilemma in Iraq," *Washington Times*, June 26, 2008. https://www3.washingtontimes.com/news/2008/jun/26/democrats-dilemma-in-iraq/. This site was accessed on January 6, 2009.

161 Eric Alterman, "Iraq: The Democrats Dilemma," *The Nation*, March 16, 2006. http://www.thenation.com/doc/20060403/alterman. This site was accessed on January 6, 2009.

162 "Obama's Iraq Dilemma," Powerline, May 31, 2008. http://www.powerlineblog.com/archives/2008/05/020650.php. This site was accessed on January 6, 2009.

163 Transcript of Democratic Presidential Candidates Debate on September 26, 2007. http://www.msnbc.msn.com/id/21013767/. This site was accessed on January 5, 2009.

164 Tim Shipman, "Barack Obama Accused of Selling Out on Iraq by Picking Hawks to Run his Foreign Policy," *Daily Telegraph*, November 27, 2008. http://www.telegraph.co.uk/news/worldnews/northamerica/usa/barackobama/3502411/Barack-Obama-accused-of-selling-out-on-Iraq-by-picking-hawks-to-run-his-foreign-policy.html. This site was accessed on January 6, 2009.

165 Ibid.

166 David E. Sanger, "Obama Tilts to Center, Inviting a Clash of Ideas," *New York Times*, November 21, 2008. http://www.nytimes.com/2008/11/22/us/politics/22assess.html?_r=1&hp. This site was accessed on January 6, 2009.

167 Brian R. Robertson, "Obama's Nixonian Dilemma with Iraq," *History News Network*, December 8, 2008. http://hnn.us/articles/57699.html. This site was accessed on January 6, 2009.

168 Ibid.

169 Text of Obama's Speech at Camp Lejeune, North Carolina, *New York Times*, February 27, 2009. http://www.nytimes.com/2009/02/27/us/politics/27obama-text.html?_r=1&ref=washington&pagewanted=all. This site was accessed on February 29, 2009.

170 Ibid.

171 Peter Baker, "With Pledges to Troops and Iraqis, Obama Details Pullout," *New York Times*, February 27, 2009. http://www.nytimes.com/2009/02/28/washington/28troops.html. This site was accessed on February 29, 2009.

172 Thomas E. Ricks, *The Gamble: General David Petraeus and the American Military Adventure in Iraq, 2006-2008* (New York: Penguin Press, 2009), 399.

173 Barack Obama, "Renewing American Leadership," *Foreign Affairs,* July/August 2007.

http://www.foreignaffairs.org/20070701faessay86401/barack-obama/renewing-american-leadership.html?mode=print. The site was accessed on December 27, 2008.

174 "The Road to the White House: How to Deal with Gaza," *Jerusalem Post*, July 5, 2007. http://cgis.jpost.com/Blogs/presidblog/entry/how_to_deal_with_gaza. The site was accessed on December 27, 2008.

175 Philip H. Gordon, "Bush's Middle East Vision," *Brookings*, Spring 2003. http://www.brookings.edu/articles/2003/spring_middleeast_gordon.aspx. The site was accessed on December 27, 2008.

176 Barack Obama, "Renewing American Leadership," *Foreign Affairs,* July/August 2007.

177 Ibid.

178 "Barack Obama Backtracks on 'Unified Jerusalem' Speech," *Reuters*, July 15, 2008. http://www.haaretz.com/hasen/spages/1001651.html. The site was accessed on December 27, 2008.

179 Prosy Delacruz's, "Obama on Iran, Syria and Jerusalem on *Jerusalem Post*," July 24, 2008. http://my.barackobama.com/page/community/post/prosydelacruz/gGx9xD. The site was accessed on December 27, 2008.

180 Aaron Lerner, "Obama and the Violated Oslo "Spirit," *IsraelInsider*, July 26, 2008. http://web.israelinsider.com/Views/13010.htm. The site was accessed on December 27, 2008.

181 David Horovitz, "Obama on Iran, Syria, and Jerusalem," *Jerusalem Post*-On line Edition, July 24, 2008. http://www.jpost.com/servlet/Satellite?cid=1215331099249&pagename=JPost%2FJPArticle%2FPrinter. The site was accessed on December 27, 2008.

182 Mark Oppenheimer, "Lets Talk," *Boston Globe*, June 22, 2008. http://www.boston.com/bostonglobe/ideas/articles/2008/06/22/lets_talk/. The site was accessed on December 28, 2008.

183 Obama-Biden, Foreign Policy. http://origin.barackobama.com/issues/foreign_policy/#iran. The site was accessed on December 28, 2008.

184 "RNC: Obama's Bad Week on Preconditions," *Reuters*, May 23, 2008. http://www.reuters.com/article/pressRelease/idUS233343+23-May-2008+PRN20080523. The site was accessed on December 28, 2008.

185 Ibid.

186 Stephen Zunes, "Barack Obama on the Middle East," *Foreign Policy in Focus,* January 10, 2008. http://www.fpif.org/fpiftxt/4886. The site was accessed on December 28, 2008.

187 Ben Smith, "Obama Team's Warring Middle East Views," *Politico*, December 6, 2008. http://dyn.politico.com/printstory.cfm?uuid=08BFFF74-18FE-70B2-A81FF1B81C5933DB. The site was accessed on December 28, 2008.

188 Eli Lake, "Conflict Zone, Will James Jones and Hillary Clinton Butt Heads Over Middle East Policy?" *New Republic*, November 26, 2008. http://www.tnr.com/politics/story.html?id=37a35a8f-5582-47fc-867c-03e8a211122f. The site was accessed on December 28, 2008.

189 Horovitz, "Obama on Iran, Syria, and Jerusalem," *Jerusalem Post*-On line Edition, July 24, 2008.

190 Ibid.

191 Steve A. Yetiv, *The Absence of Grand Strategy: The United States in the Persian Gulf, 1972-2005* (Maryland: Johns Hopkins University Press, 2008), 2.

192 Mark Tran, "Barack Obama: I will not Waste a Minute in Brokering Middle East Peace," *The Guardian*, July 23, 2008. http://www.guardian.co.uk/world/2008/jul/23/barackobama.middleeast. The site was accessed on December 28, 2008.

193 No Author, "McCain Goes After Obama on Terrorism," *Boston Globe*, June 17, 2008. http://www.boston.com/news/politics/politicalintelligence/2008/06/mccain_goes_aft.html. The site was viewed on March 9, 2009.

194 Ibid.

195 Ibid.

196 Barack Obama, "Renewing American Leadership," *Foreign Affairs*, July/August 2007. http://www.foreignaffairs.org/20070701faessay86401/barack-obama/renewing-american-leadership.html?mode=print. The site viewed on March 9, 2009.

197 Ibid.

198 For more on Bush's adoption and improvement of Clinton's strategy, see "The Evolution of American Grand Strategy and the War on Terrorism: Clinton and Bush Perspectives," in John Davis, editor, *The Global on Terrorism: Assessing the American Response* (New York: Nova Science Publishers, 2004), p. 61-79.

199 *The National Security Strategy of the United States*, The White House, September 17, 2002, 5. http://www.whitehouse.gov/nsc/nss.pdf. The site viewed on March 10, 2009.

200 For more on these organizations, see the following: John Davis, editor, *Africa and the War on Terrorism* (London: Ashgate, 2007).

201 Barack Obama, *The Audacity of Hope: Thoughts on Reclaiming the American Dream* (New York: Random House, 2006), p. 307.

202 Remarks of Senator Barack Obama on the Military Commission Legislation, September 28, 2006. http://obama.senate.gov/speech/060928-remarks_of_sena_9/index.php. The site viewed on March 10, 2009.

203 Transcript: *ABC* News/Facebook/WMUR Democratic Debate. January 5, 2008. http://abcnews.go.com/Politics/DemocraticDebate/Story?id=4092530&page=1. The site viewed on March 10, 2009.

204 Obama, "Renewing American Leadership," *Foreign Affairs*, July/August 2007.

205 Illinois Senate Debate, Illinois Radio Network October 12, 2004. http://www.ontheissues.org/Archive/Obama-Keyes_Barack_Obama.htm. The site viewed on March 10, 2009.

206 Transcript of The Democrats' Second 2008 Presidential Debate, *New York Times*, July 3, 2007. http://www.nytimes.com/2007/06/03/us/politics/03demsdebate_transcript.html. The site viewed on March 11, 2009.

207 Barack Obama in Meet the Press: Meet the Candidates 2008 series, with Tim Russert. May 4, 2008. http://www.issues2000.org/Archive/2008_Meet_the_Press_Barack_Obama.htm. The site viewed on March 11, 2009.

208 "Obama Calls Situation in Afghanistan 'Urgent,'" *CNN*, July 21, 2008. http://www.cnn.com/2008/POLITICS/07/20/obama.afghanistan/. The site viewed on March 12, 2009.

209 Transcript of the Democratic Presidential Primary debate in Iowa, August 19, 2007. http://abcnews.go.com/politics/decision2008/story?id=3498294. The site viewed on March 13, 2009.

210 Jake Tapper, "Obama Delivers Bold Speech About War on Terror-Presidential Candidate Pushes Aggressive Stance Toward Pakistan," *ABC News*, August 1, 2007. http://abcnews.go.com/Politics/story?id=3434573&page=1. The site viewed on March 13, 2009.

211 AFL-CIO Democratic Forum, FactCheck.org. August 8, 2007. http://www.factcheck.org/elections-2008/afl-cio_democratic_forum.html. The site viewed on March 13, 2009.

212 Transcript: *ABC News*/Facebook/WMUR Democratic Debate. January 5, 2008. The site viewed on March 13, 2009.

213 Heather Maher, McCain, Obama Clash On Foreign Policy At Debate," Radio Free Europe, Radio Liberty, October 8, 2008. http://www.rferl.org/Content/McCain_Obama_Clash_On_Foreign_Policy_At_Debate/1294932.html. The site viewed on March 13, 2009.

214 Obama, "Renewing American Leadership," *Foreign Affairs*, July/August 2007.

215 Michael Gordon, "Afghan Strategy Poses Stiff Challenge for Obama," *New York Times*, December 1, 2008. http://www.nytimes.com/2008/12/02/world/asia/02strategy.html?_r=1&hp. The site viewed on March 13, 2009.

216 Obama, "Renewing American Leadership," *Foreign Affairs*, July/August 2007.

217 Text of President Obama's Remarks on New Strategy for Afghanistan and Pakistan, *New York Times*, March 27, 2009. http://www.nytimes.com/2009/03/27/us/politics/27obama-text.html?_r=1&sq=text%20of%20Obama&st=cse&%2339;s%20Afghanistan%20strategy=&scp=1&pagewanted=all. The site viewed on March 27, 2009.

218 Ibid.

219 Obama, "Renewing American Leadership," *Foreign Affairs*, July/August 2007.

220 India is 'Top Priority' for Barack Obama," *South Asian Post*, October 30 2008. http://www.southasianpost.com/portal2/c1ee8c441d4a4790011d4ef802b101d9_India_is__top_priority__for_Barack_Obama.do.html. The site viewed on March 27, 2009.

221 Text of President Obama's Remarks on New Strategy for Afghanistan and Pakistan, *New York Times*, March 27, 2009.

222 Jeremy Page in Mumbai, Tom Coghlan and Zahid Hussain, "Mumbai Attacks 'Were a Ploy to Wreck Obama Plan to Isolate Al Qaeda,'" *TimesOnline*, December 1, 2008. http://www.timesonline.co.uk/tol/news/world/asia/article5263919.ece?&EMC-Bltn=IMYAX9. The site viewed on March 27, 2009.

223 Obama, "Renewing American Leadership," *Foreign Affairs*, July/August 2007.

224 Gary Kamiya, "Why Obama Should End the "War on Terror," *Salon*, November 25, 2008. http://www.salon.com/opinion/kamiya/2008/11/25/obama_war_on_terror/. The site viewed on March 27, 2009.

225 Ibid.

226 "America's Image Slips, But Allies Share US Concerns Over Iran, Hamas," Pew Global Attitudes Project, June 13, 2006. http://pewglobal.org/reports/display.php?PageID=825. The site viewed on March 27, 2009.

227 "Remarks of Senator Obama: The War We Need to Win," Wilson Center, Washington, D.C., August 1, 2007. http://www.barackobama.com/2007/08/01/the_war_we_need_to_win.php. The site viewed on March 27, 2009.

228 Ibid.

229 During the campaign Obama made a statement that illustrated his lack of knowledge on two of the more successful components of Bush's strategy in the war on terror. Obama's statement is as follows: "As President, I will create a Shared Security Partnership Program to forge an international intelligence and law enforcement infrastructure to take down terrorist

networks from the remote islands of Indonesia, to the sprawling cities of Africa. This program will provide $5 billion over three years for counter-terrorism cooperation with countries around the world, including information sharing, funding for training, operations, border security, anti-corruption programs, technology, and targeting terrorist financing. And this effort will focus on helping our partners succeed without repressive tactics, because brutality breeds terror, it does not defeat it." Statement taken from "Remarks of Senator Obama: The War We Need to Win."

230 Ibid.

231 No author, "Growth of Al Qaeda Safe Havens 'Troubling' Pentagon," *Arab Times*, May 25, 2008. http://www.arabtimesonline.com/pdf08/may/25/page%2001.pdf. The site viewed on March 27, 2009.

232 Stephen Walt, "Two Cheers for Clinton's Foreign Policy," *Foreign Affairs*, March/April 2000. http://www.foreignaffairs.org/20000301faessay28/stephen-m-walt/two-cheers-for-clinton-s-foreign-policy.html. This site was viewed on January 13, 2009.

233 Richard N. Haass, "The Squandered Presidency: Demanding More from the Commander in Chief," *Foreign Affairs*, May/June 2000. http://www.foreignaffairs.org/20000501faresponse50/richard-n-haass/the-squandered-presidency-demanding-more-from-the-commander-in-chief.html. This site was viewed on January 13, 2009.

234 Stephen Lendman, "Obama Mania," *Baltimore Chronicle*, November 10, 2008. http://www.baltimorechronicle.com/2008/111008Lendman.shtml. This site was viewed on January 13, 2009.

235 Barack Obama, "Renewing American Leadership," *Foreign Affairs*, July/August 2007. http://www.foreignaffairs.org/20070701faessay86401/barack-obama/renewing-american-leadership.html?mode=print. This site was viewed on January 13, 2009.

236 The reader may wish to consult a fantastic book that provides another perspective about the impact of the inherited phenomenon; David Sanger, *The Inheritance: The World Obama Confronts and the Challenges to American Power* (New York: Harmony Books, 2009).

237 Michael Mandelbaum, "Foreign Policy as Social Work," *Foreign Affairs*, January/February 1996. http://www.foreignaffairs.org/19960101faessay4169/michael-mandelbaum/foreign-policy-as-social-work.html. This site was viewed on January 13, 2009.